MW00655283

THE MAKING

OF A

WATCHMAN

Practical Training for Prophetic Prayer and Powerful Intercession

JENNIFER LECLAIRE

DESTINY IMAGE® PUBLISHERS, INC.
P.O. Box 310, Shippensburg, PA 17257-0310
"Promoting Inspired Lives."

This book and all other Destiny Image and Destiny Image Fiction books are available at Christian bookstores and distributors worldwide.

Cover design by Eileen Rockwell

For more information on foreign distributors, call 717-532-3040.

Reach us on the Internet: www.destinyimage.com.

ISBN 13 TP: 978-0-7684-5600-4

ISBN 13 eBook: 978-0-7684-5615-8

ISBN 13 HC: 978-0-7684-5617-2

ISBN 13 LP: 978-0-7684-5616-5

For Worldwide Distribution.

1 2 3 4 5 6 7 8 / 25 24 23 22 21

DEDICATION

This book is dedicated to those who are picking up the baton from the generation of generals that plowed through so much persecution to bring us present-day truth—and to those generals who are willing to pour their lives out as a drink offering to that generation in a changing of the guard. The generational synergy is only possible by both groups locking arms in unity for the purposes of Christ in the earth.

ACKNOWLEDGMENTS

Thanks to Larry Sparks and Destiny Image for seeing the need for a new book on the watchman for a new era of Christianity. I'm grateful for the pioneers who laid such a strong foundation to build on for a new season of gross darkness and great glory that is before us.

CONTENTS

BY CINDY JACOBS

I am so glad that I was the one who was asked to write the foreword to this much-needed book, *The Making of a Watchman*. The author, Jennifer LecClaire, has been used by God to write a training manual that gives a clarion call to all generations that God has called us to stand in the gap upon the wall and sound the alarm about potential dangers.

Some people simply do not know what to do when they have a vision or impression of impending disasters, or potential problems that can be averted. It may be that they do not understand "why" they have had a certain dream or warning. Even after books have been written about dreams and intercessory prayer, many people still believe that a dream is like fate. They are being shown something of the future, but it is going to happen no matter what.

Not so! Thank God for this instructive book that gives knowledge and practical steps on how to be a watchman. It also helps the reader to realize the need to both intercede over, and sometimes give a warning to someone about their dream.

This book is much needed and Jennifer does an outstanding job in giving clarity both for the need for and the how-tos of being a watchman. She is especially skilled at starting with the basics on being called to be a watchman, discerning the call, functioning as a watchman, as well as giving warnings.

I remember prophesying over a woman at a church in California, when God gave me an unusual word for her. She was standing in a prayer line when I stopped in front of her and suddenly blurted out, "Where is your husband?" She replied that he was a traveling salesman and was away. I immediately gave what was almost a command, "Call your husband and tell him to go to the hospital right now and get checked out." The lady was shocked, and frankly, it kind of shocked me too. The Holy Spirit through the warning was quite adamant!

Because she trusted me as a prophet, she called her husband right away and shared with him what I had said. He replied that he felt fine, but at the word of the Lord, and, I might add, his wife's strong urging, went right to an emergency room to be checked. To his surprise, the doctor found that he was bleeding internally and might have died if they had not found the source of the bleeding when they did.

Being a watchman is a responsibility. I recall another time when an intercessor had a dream that a friend of hers had a brain tumor. She called her and and asked her to go to the doctor for a scan. It ended up that they found a tumor in her brain and were able to operate on it and save the woman's life because they caught it when they did.

One of the chapters that I love in *The Making of a Watchman* is entitled, "Cultivating a Watchman's Eye." To quote from Jennifer, she says, "Most of us know how to pray. Fewer understand the mechanics of watching in the spirit." She encourages us to learn how to use our ability as a watchman so we can discern spiritual activity around us while walking through our everyday lives.

The best watchmen are the ones with acute spiritual eyesight. One might be in the grocery store and then, suddenly, we are arrested by the Holy Spirit to pray or give a warning. One day I was in the grocery store and felt I needed to go stand in a certain aisle and wait there. For what, I didn't know.

After a bit, I started feeling kind of foolish for just standing there. At last, I saw a friend of mine that I knew from church come up the aisle. All of a sudden, with my watchman's eyes, I knew that she was in big trouble.

I approached her and greeted her and then said, "How are things at home with your marriage?" She looked kind of strange and glanced around furtively. I felt to probe her a bit deeper. At last, in a low voice, she whispered, "My husband gets angry at me." I pushed some more and replied in a voice to match hers, "Is he beating you?"

All of a sudden, I knew she needed to get out of the house right away! I mean, just flee for her life. I beseeched her, "Alice (not her real name), do you have any place to go for a while?" Again, she was quite evasive and I stressed, "Please, please leave!" "Miss Cindy, I just can't, I just can't," she moaned in obvious despair.

She left and hurried away. Shortly after, I heard that her husband had whipped a gun out at their house while playing poker with his friends and shot her dead. I mourned over that news.

All you can do is warn. Sometimes they don't take the warning, but you did your job as a watchman.

Jennifer helps us to understand the need to wait on God in our times of intercession. Sometimes in your prayer times, you will just sit and wait in the presence of God. We need times of "listening prayer" in order for God to talk to us, as well as our continually talking to Him.

She quotes from her book, *The Seer Dimensions* that "Silence is the foundation of contemplative prayer. Contemplative prayer opens your eyes in ways other prayer does not because it leads you into intimacy with God."

A number of people have asked me questions on being a watchman through the years. I wish I had had this book on *The Making of a*

Watchman years ago to recommend to them. It is comprehensive and answers many of the questions that people need to know in order to live the life of a watchman, which is one of our Christian duties.

You are about to embark on a great spiritual adventure! Open these pages and be led on a journey with the Holy Spirit that will change the way you live your life

—**Cindy Jacobs**
Generals International
Dallas, Texas

Chapter 1

CALLING ALL WATCHMEN

THE Lord is calling a new generation of watchmen. He's calling those who can learn from the watchmen of yesterday while watching right now and preparing the watchmen of tomorrow. There's a changing of the guard under way and God is looking for fresh eyes to watch and diverse voices to pray.

Modern watchmen will be soccer moms and CEOs. Contemporary watchmen will be elementary school students and grocery store clerks. In a new era of the prophetic movement, God is pulling from all walks of life and making, shaping, and molding the willing into wise watchmen who will pull from treasures old and new (see Matt. 13:52). I hear the Lord saying:

> Awake, watchmen. Rise from your positions in home-places and marketplaces and other places and get on your posts. Watch and pray, for the hour is at hand for some of the most significant events in human history to unfold. I am calling you forth, indeed, for such as time as this.
>
> Stand on your watchtower and wait to see what I will say to you. Then sound the alarm and pray it through.

> Stand and watch. Watch and pray. Pray and trumpet My
> warnings in the nations of the earth. I have called you
> to be My watchers, so don't stop looking and don't stop
> speaking forth what you see, and don't stop standing in
> the gap to stop the enemy forces from gaining a foothold
> in your city. We are in this together.

God is indeed calling watchmen from all walks of life. I don't believe that's anything new. God always works with the willing. And He has lots of experience taking everyday people and making them into watchmen for His glory. In this hour, there is a dearth of watchmen even while enemy activity is raging and revival is on the horizon. If you are reading this book, you may be part of the company of new-breed watchmen God is calling forth in this generation.

WHAT EXACTLY IS A WATCHMAN?

Sometimes in the Body of Christ we hear words tossed around but we don't truly know their meaning. The word *watchman* is only used twenty-two times in the New King James Version of the Bible, but the function of watching is used *dozens* of times more.

God has had watchmen in place at least since the days of Moses in the Exodus. Although Scripture doesn't use the word *watchman*, it does speak of the morning watch in Exodus 14:24. Clearly, there was a watchman in place because you can't have a watch without a watchman. And although the word *watchman* is not used in the New Testament, the operation did not expire after the Book of Malachi. Watchmen were vital to kingdom operations in the Old and New Testaments and they are just as critical to Kingdom operations today.

Let's back up for a minute and answer this question: What is a watchman? When we discuss the role of a watchman in Chapter Three, we'll look at the many expressions tied up in this one operation. For now, we'll look at the simplest definition. *Merriam-Webster*'s dictionary defines *watchman* as "a person who keeps watch: guard." Synonyms for *watchman* are "keeper, lookout, minder, sentinel, and watcher." Biblically speaking, *The International Standard Bible Encyclopedia* defines *watchman* as "used to designate a sentinel on the city walls...or on the hilltops."

In short, watchmen are prophets, prophetic people, intercessors, and others who watch in the spirit for three specific activities: what the enemy is doing, what angels are doing, and what God is doing. Not all watchmen are prophets, but all prophets have a watchman function. In fact, God intends for all believers to have a watchman function, even if it is just watching over their own life, their family, or their business. Remember, Jesus called us all to "watch and pray" (Matt. 26:41).

Many people want to blame God when viruses spread across the earth and when terror attacks wreak havoc in the nations—or even when something bad happens in their church, business, or family. While there are principles in Scripture—such as reaping what you sow, the law of sin and death, and the free will of mankind to do evil—God has given us more authority than we realize. God doesn't *make* bad things happen to good people. Much of what happens in the earth realm could be stopped by a man or woman who stands in the gap to pray. However, that requires a watchman to see what is coming in the spirit before it manifests in the natural.

I love what Dutch Sheets wrote in his important book *Watchman Prayer*:

Protection from the attacks of our enemy—even for believers—is not automatic. There is a part for us to play. Though God is sovereign, this does not mean He is literally in control of everything that happens. He has left much to the decisions and actions of humankind. *...God's plan is to warn or alert us to Satan's tactics.* This is deduced from the simple fact that, since God says not to be *unaware* of Satan's tactics, He must be willing to make us *aware* of them. ...If these attacks were always going to be obvious, alertness would not be necessary.[1]

James Goll, author of *Lifestyle of a Watchman*, urges all believers to embrace the watchman anointing and mandate in their life. He says:

Each of us has been chosen to be a watchman of the Lord in this generation. It is a calling. An assignment. And in whatever ways God calls you to pray, it should be a very strategic appointment on your calendar. ...God seems to be strategically calling His people to prayer watches as never before.[2]

Throughout church history, watchmen have been underappreciated, misunderstood, ignored, and at times persecuted. Now more than ever, God is calling watchmen on the wall to look out for signs of the times, to spy out the enemy's plans, to keep watch in intercession. Now more than ever, God is calling watchmen to observe what He is doing so they can report coming outpourings so the Body of Christ can get into agreement with the King of Glory.

Before we move into the depths of the call of the watchman, let's look at some historic and modern-day watchmen who have paved the way for us. Some passed the torch of watchman prayer to others. Some will pass the torch to us so the fire on the altar never goes out (see Lev. 6:13).

REES HOWELLS: A WARTIME WATCHMAN

Rees Howells goes down in 20th-century history as a watchman intercessor who helped save the United Kingdom from the Nazis' reign of terror in World War II. In his personal journal, he wrote, "I want to know that the Holy Spirit is stronger than the devil in the Nazi system. This is the battle of the ages, and victory for millions of people."[3]

God trained Howells for years before the war broke out. He was head of the Bible College of Wales during those dark days, but he fearlessly led prayer watches that contributed to the defeat of an evil regime. He wrote, "The world became our parish and we were led to be responsible to intercede for countries and nations."[4]

Gloom and doom media headlines did not deter the faith of this watchman intercessor. Howells and his students-turned-intercessors held prayer watches day and night to push back the powers of darkness. The Holy Spirit assured Howells that the college was under God's protection from enemy air attacks. He wrote:

There have been so many places bombed in London, even Buckingham Palace has been touched. I was burdened to pray for the King and Queen, and I believe our prayer will be answered. I am just watching how God will take hold of the enemy.[5]

Notice Howells said he was watching how God would take hold of the enemy. He was watching. He was praying. What followed goes down in history as the Miracle at Dunkirk.

Hundreds of thousands of British and French soldiers were trapped on the beaches in Dunkirk, France, in 1940. The Nazis were poised to wipe them out when, unexplainably, Adolf Hitler gave a halt order to the armored columns moving toward the soldiers. About 400,000 soldiers were rescued in Operation Dynamo, which was surely an answer to the intercession of Howells and many under his oversight at the college (as well as intercession around the world). Hitler surrendered.

WATCHMAN NEE: LIVING AND DYING FOR CHRIST

Though his parents named him Henry, Watchman Nee was born as a watchman and is remembered as such. Nee got saved in mainland China in 1920 and wrote scores of publications on spiritual maturity and prayer. He was imprisoned in 1952 and died there thirty years later. According to his biography, he considered himself to be a watchman raised up to sound out a warning call in the dark night.

Nee was an equipper who focused, among other things, on teaching believers to pray and engage in spiritual warfare. Like a true watchman, he wrote:

To remove warfare from a spiritual life is to render it unspiritual. Life in the spirit is a suffering way, filled with watching and laboring, burdened by weariness and trial, punctuated by heartbreak and conflict. It is a life utterly outpoured entirely for the kingdom of God and lived in complete disregard for one's personal happiness.[6]

He also left us this wisdom:

How we need the Lord to enlighten our eyes that we may comprehend afresh the importance of prayer and know anew its value. Furthermore, we must recognize that had Satan not deceived us, we would not be neglecting prayer so much. We should therefore watch and discover therein all the various wiles of Satan. We will not allow him to delude us any more in relaxing in prayer.[7]

Again, Watchman Nee fully embraced his calling, to the point of changing his name. The Chinese name *Duo Sheng* means "watchman" in English. But it has a richer meaning in Chinese, meaning "sound of the gong" or "a watchman to raise the people of God to service."

What should we take away from this watchman's life and death? Nee was committed to watching, praying, fighting—and fulfilling the Great Commission. He was truly a pioneering watchman in China and paid a heavy price for releasing his voice against the denominationalism in the nation that eventually turned to communistic, antichrist rule.

LANCE LAMBERT: A WATCHMAN FOR ISRAEL

Lance Lambert went home to be with the Lord in 2015. British by birth, he goes down in church history as a watchman for Israel. Lambert discovered his Jewish ancestry and became an Israeli citizen in 1980. Known for his eschatological views, he walked in the ministry tradition of Watchman Nee and T. Austin-Sparks. He wrote a book challenging Christians to take their place as intercessors for Israel.

Five years before his death, Lambert released a prophecy in true watchman style that is worth noting here:

Do not fear neither be dismayed for that which is coming upon the face of the earth, for I am with you. Nevertheless, I have a serious controversy with the nations. They are seeking to divide My Land, the land that I covenanted to give to Abraham and to his seed after him through Isaac and Jacob, as an everlasting inheritance. This I will not allow without devastating judgment upon those nations who pursue this plan.

I have arisen with intense and furious anger and will not back down until I have destroyed their well-being. I will cause their economies to fail, and their financial system to break down, and even the climate to fail them! I will turn them upside down and inside out, and they will not know what has hit them, whether they be super powers or not. For I am the only One, the Almighty God and besides Me there is none to compare.

Do they believe that in their arrogance they can contradict and nullify covenants that I the Almighty have made? Do they believe that they can change what has gone forth from My mouth with impunity? It is My Word and My decree that has gone forth concerning the seed of Abraham. It will not be changed by man. I and I alone am Almighty. Do not fear! For this reason, a new and a far more serious phase of judgment is commencing.

Do not fear. It is I who is shaking all things. Remember that in Me you have peace, but in the world tribulation. Trust Me! I am shaking all things so that which cannot be shaken may remain. When all your circumstances become abnormal, discover in Me your peace, your rest and your fulfillment. In this phase the old and powerful nations will become as if they are third world countries: super powers will no longer be super powers but countries such as India and China will arise to take their place. A great company of the redeemed will come out of these two countries. In all this change, do not fear.

I know your weakness and your tendency to fear, but do not be dismayed at these things. In the midst of all this shaking, this turmoil and strife, there are two peoples that lie at its heart: the true and living church and Israel. I will use these matters, these events, to purify one and to save the other! Do not fear, above the storms, the shaking, and the conflict, I am the Everlasting and Almighty One. In Me you cannot be shaken; you can only lose what is not worth holding![18]

LEONARD RAVENHILL: THE CHALLENGING WATCHMAN

Leonard Ravenhill was born in Leeds, England. He goes down in church history for a bold voice with rhythmic truths who warns man of the consequences of disobedience to God. He warned the church repeatedly about lukewarm attitudes, prayerlessness, and the like. In short, he confronted sin in the church. His book *Why Revival Tarries* is a classic.

Ravenhill warned us entertainment is the devil's substitute for joy and wondered how we can pull down satan's strongholds if we don't have the strength to turn off the TV. He mourned over how the early church was married to poverty, prisons, and persecutions, while the modern church is married to prosperity, personality, and popularity. He bemoaned that the church has more fashion than passion, is more pathetic than prophetic, and is more superficial than supernatural. He wrote these words:

No man is greater than his prayer life. The pastor who is not praying is playing; the people who are not praying are straying. ...We have many organizers, but few agonizers; many players and payers, few pray-ers; many singers, few clingers; lots of pastors, few wrestlers; many fears, few tears; much fashion, little passion; many interferers, few intercessors; many writers, but few fighters. Failing here, we fail everywhere.[9]

DAVID WILKERSON: A WEEPING WATCHMAN

Some will remember him for his books, like *The Cross and the Switch-blade*, which became a best-selling phenomenon with more than 15 million copies sold in over 30 languages. Others will remember him for launching Teen Challenge, a nationwide ministry to reach out to people with life-controlling habits. Still others will remember Wilkerson for his sometimes-controversial prophetic words. He was truly a watchman for his generation, and taught a lot about the watchman. He went home to be with the Lord after a car crash in April 2011.

Over and over again, Wilkerson issued warning messages with heart-felt prayers. His last message to the American church was spine-chilling. He spoke of a "noted televangelist" who gave a shocking warning to the United States. He called him a "respected" man we know and who is warning America that there's coming a catastrophe that's going to cost the lives of multitudes and change the way we live forever. He also pointed to many praying pastors who prophesied along these lines.

Something is coming shortly, something coming soon and we had better be prepared. ...Something is telling the whole world that it's on the brink of a catastrophe. These are secular people. This intu-itiveness of even the most wicked on the face of the earth...they know something has happened and they dread to talk about it. There's a fear.[10]

Wilkerson was bold in his warnings. He once warned the Assemblies of God, the denomination he served, about preaching a gospel of accommodation instead of a pure gospel:

> I am not coming to you as a pastor but with a prophetic word. God so shook me recently with this message that I should bring it somewhere, sometime in Springfield. This morning the Lord, by His Spirit, spoke to my heart that this is the time. He has called me to be one of His watchmen, and I have wept over this and prayed that He will help me deliver the message in a spirit of love. This is not a chastisement but a warning for the Assemblies of God.[11]

STEVE HILL: A REVIVALIST WITH A WATCHMAN'S HEART

Steve Hill came on the scene as a fireball preaching at the Brownsville Revival, but he was a true watchman in his generation. Like his mentors Leonard Ravenhill and David Wilkerson, he was known for strong warnings to the church. Many of his warning were about candy-coated gospels and false teachings.

He went home to be with the Lord in 2014, but not before releasing one of his most pivotal books, *The Spiritual Avalanche That Could Kill Millions*. The book was based on a vision he had of skiers on a mountain when an avalanche hit. The avalanche was false teaching. He wrote:

> The layers upon layers of snow have been steadily covering the solid, traditional truth of Christ. God's Word tells us that foolish teaching in these days will become so fashionable even the most dedicated believer can become deceived... (Matt. 24:24). It's happening

before our eyes. One spiritual leader said the other day, "You guys are old-fashioned 'holiness.' We are modern-day 'grace.' You live in bondage, while we can do anything we want."

Pastors and teachers worldwide have succumbed to heretical teachings, including universal reconciliation, deification of man, challenging the validity of the Word of God including His judgments, and even lifting any boundaries, claiming His amazing grace is actually "amazing freedom." You are free to live according to your own desires. Sound familiar? "In those days there was no king in Israel; everyone did what was right in his own eyes" (Judg. 17:6). Many popular, self-proclaimed ministers of the gospel are covering the slopes and will be held accountable for the spiritual death of millions.

Just as the ski patrol did in this vision, those who are aware of what's happening must take swift and accurate action. Their weapons of warfare must be aimed at the peaks and the avalanche terrain to dispel the lies. Apostles, prophets, evangelists, pastors, and teachers must be willing to drop spiritual bombs, fire anti-heresy missiles, and even drive into the danger zones armed with explosive truth to confront this potential avalanche. The spiritual generals of this generation must leave the war room and put their years of experience on the front lines.[12]

DICK EASTMAN: AN EVANGELISM-MINDED WATCHMAN

Dick Eastman, international president of Every Home for Christ, is an evangelism-minded watchman. He has traveled the globe over 100 times with the gospel of Jesus Christ. In fact, God gave Eastman a prophetic promise in his prayer closet about seeing millions of souls come to the Kingdom through his ministry. That was back in 1964.

Eastman joined Every Home for Christ and launched a Change the World School of Prayer that gathered people from over 100 denominations to teach prayer within a few years. Over 3 million people in 120 nations—including the likes of Mike Bickle and Lou Engle—have participated in Dick's prayer schools all over the world. His book *The Hour That Changes the World* has sold 1.5 million copies globally.

From the Gap Prayer Room, intercession is lifted up to heaven Monday through Friday from 6 a.m. to midnight and Saturday 8 a.m. to midnight. Inside the Watchman Training Center is the Watchman Wall, which serves as a symbol that aims to inspire intercession. There are 12 small rooms within the wall called prayer grottos where up to five people can make intercession using prayer and worship tools. Meanwhile, the Harp and Bowl Prayer Rooms are dedicated solely to prayer and the Watchman Training Center hosts large prayer and worship gatherings, the monthly school of prayer, and a weekly commission service.

In his book *A Watchman's Guide to Praying God's Promises* he writes:

If you are both a watchman and a prayer leader, I urge you to build a Wall of Prayer even if it requires many months to establish a complete Wall. Keep in mind that a Wall of Prayer doesn't necessarily mean 24/7 "on-site" prayer, but people keeping their watch faithfully wherever they are. They do this in order that continuous prayer will rise day and night in a particular community or region. Of course, on-site prayer can be a part of this, and whenever such is possible it is highly recommended and encouraged.

As you begin your role as a watchman I challenge you with the words of two great intercessors from past generations. S. D.

Gordon, a Bible teacher a century ago in Boston, declared, "The great people of the earth are the people who pray. Prayer isn't the only thing, but it is the chief thing." To this we add the provocative statement of inspired devotional writer Oswald Chambers: "Prayer isn't merely preparation for the work. Prayer is the work!"[13]

DUTCH SHEETS: AN ALL-AMERICAN WATCHMAN

Dutch Sheets is a modern-day watchman who has birthed movements of intercessors who watch and pray. His heart is to see America experience a sweeping revival and return to its godly heritage. He encourages people to contend for awakening and wrote the perennial book *Watchman Prayer: Protecting Your Family, Home and Community from the Enemy's Schemes*. In this book, he wrote what I feel are appropriate words to end this chapter. I could not have put it better myself:

> I challenge you to make a difference. Learn the power of prayer and apply the principles of the watchman. We must take back the portions Satan has seized in our nation and around the world. Let's become spiritually militant and aggressive as we deal with the serpent and his stealing, killing and destroying. Let there be no more agnostics where Satan is concerned. Let's expose and stop him! Let's get him out of our gardens![14]

Are you ready to watch? Are you part of a new generation of watchman who will stand, look out, and make intercession? If so, read on. The pages that follow will educate, inspire, equip, and launch you into your calling.

NOTES

1. Dutch Sheets, *Watchman Prayer* (Bloomington, MN: Chosen Books, 2019), 21.

2. James W. Goll, "You Are Chosen as a Spiritual Watchman," God Encounters Today, 2017, https://www.charismamag.com/blogs/a-voice-calling-out/32375-james-goll-you-are-chosen-as-a-spiritual-watchman.

3. Norman Grubb, *Rees Howells: Intercessor*, 274.

4. Ibid., 273.

5. Ibid.

6. Watchman Nee, *The Spiritual Man* (New York, NY: Christian Fellowship Publishers, 1968), 66.

7. Watchman Nee, *The Prayer Ministry of the Church* (New York, NY: Christian Fellowship Publishers, 1973), 113.

8. Lance Lambert, qtd. in Neville Johnson, "From Neville Johnson," Sidroth.org, May 19, 2010, https://sidroth.org/articles/neville-johnson.

9. Leonard Ravenhill, *Why Revival Tarries* (Bloomington, MN: Bethany House Publishers, 1987), 25.

10. David Wilkerson, "That Dreadful Day," March 25, 2009, https://youtu.be/bRn3UznKjAE.

11. David Wilkerson, "The Dangers of The Gospel of Accommodation," accessed September 30, 2020, http://www.gfellowship.com/david-wilkersons-warning-to-the-assemblies-of-god.html.

12. Steve Hill, *Spiritual Avalanche: The Threat of False Teachings that Could Destroy Millions* (Lake Mary, FL: Charisma House, 2013), 7-8.

13. Dick Eastman, *A Watchman's Guide to Praying God's Promises* (Colorado Springs, CO: Every Home for Christ, 2012), 8-9.

14. Dutch Sheets, *Watchman Prayer: Protecting Your Family, Home and Community from the Enemy's Schemes* (Bloomington, MN: Chosen Books, 2008), 24.

Chapter 2

DISCERNING THE CALL
OF A WATCHMAN

I was in the barracks on the campus of an orphanage in Nicaragua. I came in late at night after shooting a documentary, so everyone else was fast asleep. I tiptoed around the barracks trying my level best not to disturb anyone as I prepared for some much-needed rest. Exhausted, I climbed up to the top bunk and situated my mosquito net securely. The only sounds I could hear were snoring women and iguanas scurrying across the tin roof above us.

Even though I was worn out physically, my spirit would not settle. I lay in my bed, quietly praying in the 90-degree heat, when the still small voice of the Lord told me to read Ezekiel 3. Two years old in the Lord, I had not yet read Ezekiel and had no idea what to expect. I grabbed my travel Bible and a small flashlight and opened the Scriptures to Ezekiel 3. The header in the New King James Version reads, "The Responsibility of the Prophet."

I devoured the words with hunger as God told Ezekiel to "Eat this scroll, and go, speak to the house of Israel" (Ezek. 3:1). I kept on reading as God flat out told Ezekiel the people would not listen to him, and that God would make his forehead strong against their foreheads because they were so heard-hearted (see Ezek. 2:7-9). I kept on reading as the Spirit of God transported Ezekiel to Tel Abib, to his amazement (see Ezek. 7:12-15). (You can read more about being transported in the spirit in my book, *The Seer Dimensions*.)

All of this was intriguing, and if I had stopped reading there in the middle of that hot night with a fine-print Bible in the dark with a flashlight, I would have missed what God was saying. If I hadn't decided to, as Bethel's Bill Johnson often says, "keep reading until God speaks," I would not have received the revelation God was waiting to pour out. I kept on reading and saw the next section heading read, "Ezekiel Is a Watchman."

MY CALLING AS A WATCHMAN

When I read Ezekiel 3:17, the words jumped off the page: "Son of man, I have made you a watchman for the house of Israel; therefore hear a word from My mouth, and give them warning from Me." I had never even heard of a watchman at my young age in the Lord. I read the entire passage in Ezekiel 3:17-21:

> *Son of man, I have made you a watchman for the house of Israel; therefore hear a word from My mouth, and give them warning from Me: When I say to the wicked, "You shall surely die," and you give him no warning, nor speak to warn the wicked from his wicked way, to save his life, that same wicked man shall die in his iniquity; but his blood I will require at your hand. Yet, if you warn the wicked, and*

he does not turn from his wickedness, nor from his wicked way, he shall die in his iniquity; but you have delivered your soul.

Again, when a righteous man turns from his righteousness and commits iniquity, and I lay a stumbling block before him, he shall die; because you did not give him warning, he shall die in his sin, and his righteousness which he has done shall not be remembered; but his blood I will require at your hand. Nevertheless if you warn the righteous man that the righteous should not sin, and he does not sin, he shall surely live because he took warning; also you will have delivered your soul.

I was without words. That was a heavy passage. How could one man be responsible for such a tremendous life-or-death task? How could God put that weight of obligation on a single prophet, especially when He already made it clear that the people would not listen to him? Surely, there would be persecution from these hard-hearted Israelites. Certainly, there would be suffering in this mandate. The spirit of the fear of the Lord rested upon me as I read those verses, but I kept reading until the end of the chapter.

With slivers of moonlight peering through the open windows—and iguanas prancing back and forth over the hot tin roof—I lay in my bed with a troubled soul. What could this mean? Why would the Lord have me sitting in the second-poorest country in the Americas in the middle of the night with a flashlight reading these passages? I didn't ponder this long before He told me, again in that still small voice almost as if not to wake up the other missionaries, "Read Ezekiel 33."

CONFIRMING THE CALLING

Perhaps because I wasn't getting it, God sent me thirty chapters down the line to Ezekiel 33. I started reading in verse one and the storyline got more intense. Ezekiel 33:1-9 shook me:

> *Again the word of the Lord came to me, saying, "Son of man, speak to the children of your people, and say to them: 'When I bring the sword upon a land, and the people of the land take a man from their territory and make him their watchman, when he sees the sword coming upon the land, if he blows the trumpet and warns the people, then whoever hears the sound of the trumpet and does not take warning, if the sword comes and takes him away, his blood shall be on his own head. He heard the sound of the trumpet, but did not take warning; his blood shall be upon himself. But he who takes warning will save his life. But if the watchman sees the sword coming and does not blow the trumpet, and the people are not warned, and the sword comes and takes any person from among them, he is taken away in his iniquity; but his blood I will require at the watchman's hand.'*
>
> *"So you, son of man: I have made you a watchman for the house of Israel; therefore you shall hear a word from My mouth and warn them for Me. When I say to the wicked, 'O wicked man, you shall surely die!' and you do not speak to warn the wicked from his way, that wicked man shall die in his iniquity; but his blood I will require at your hand. Nevertheless if you warn the wicked to turn from his way, and he does not turn from his way, he shall die in his iniquity; but you have delivered your soul."*

And that's when I got it. God was calling me as a watchman. He confirmed the call by showing me twice—a double mention. I didn't know what to do with this revelation. I didn't know how to step into that role. I didn't tell anyone about it. I was almost hoping it would go away. But soon, the Lord started giving me words of warning and they were like fire shut up in my bones until I released them. I accepted the call as a watchman.

SIGNS YOU MAY BE A WATCHMAN

Shortly after my calling to serve the Kingdom as a watchman, God also called me as a prophet. Not all watchmen are prophets, but all prophets should have a watchman function. In fact, every believer is called to watch and pray. But a believer or a prophet or an intercessor with a strong watchman thrust will feel led to watch and pray frequently.

I believe God is giving more people a watchman anointing in this hour. Your call as a watchman may not be as dramatic as mine. Not everyone who is called has dramatic encounters. But there are clear signs you may have a watchman anointing.

You receive frequent words of warning from the Lord.

Although the watchman can release words of comfort and alert us of God's presence in its many manifestations, watchmen are not watchmen if they aren't expressing warnings. Indeed, releasing warnings is the primary function of a watchman, followed closely by intercession. The warning drives the intercession, but sometimes the intercession drives the warning.

When God first called me into prophetic ministry with this watchman thrust, the only thing I was hearing from the Lord were warnings. It wasn't pleasant because people grew weary of my coming. The warnings were so frequent that when the pastor saw me walking toward him, he started heading in the opposite direction because he didn't want to hear what I had to say. I'm being somewhat glib, but the reality is that everyone knew what came out of my mouth in a prophetic council meeting was going to be a warning.

I'll always remember the warning dream right before a major conference. In the dream, we were in the sanctuary having service when three men walked right through the door, through the lobby, and down the left-hand side of the sanctuary. They were wearing all black, including black cowboy hats. No one seemed to notice them but me, and no one stopped them. They went straight back to the children's ministry area behind the double doors at the rear of the building. It was clear to me that some danger was targeting the children's ministry during the conference. We put additional protocols in place to prevent that from occurring.

Leadership heeded my warnings, but at that time I did not have much to share beyond warnings of danger. Part of the reason for this unbalanced expression was my environment and what I had been taught. I was in a spiritual warfare church. The warfare was constant; therefore, the Lord was showing me what the leadership needed to see, but I didn't have the training to do much more with it.

Three things changed that. I moved on from this church, which was seemingly always under heavy fire and rarely taught about anything but demonology. Therefore, the frequency of the warnings waned. Second, as I matured in this gift I understood watchmen should also watch for the Lord and His angels, as well as other positive developments. Third, I grew in intimacy with the Lord, which enabled me to discern His presence more readily.

You carry prayer burdens in association with the warning.

Some erroneously teach that the watchman's responsibility stops when he blows the trumpet or sounds the alarm. In other words, they relegate the watchman to a mere messenger to deliver a warning. But that's only part of the biblical watchman's function. If God gave you the warning, it should come with an intercessory prayer burden. The watchman's function, then, is to watch and pray—and, when led by the Spirit, to mobilize other intercessors.

God is always looking for people to intercede in times of trouble. Ezekiel 22:30 reveals the heart of God: "So I sought for a man among them who would make a wall, and stand in the gap before Me on behalf of the land, that I should not destroy it; but I found no one." God sends a warning so that the enemy's plans can be averted through fervent intercession. The watchman must become part of, if not lead, the intercessory prayer team. Watchmen carry a true intercessory prayer burden until the enemy's plans are quashed.

You feel fire in your bones to release the warning.

When a watchman receives a warning, it almost consumes him until he releases it. It's not a passing feeling; it's a true fire. There's an urgency in your spirit to release it. This urgency comes from the Lord. It's part of the cloak of zeal in Isaiah 59:17.

We see this urgency in Jeremiah's ministry. This prophet's ministry was unpopular, and typically the modern watchman's ministry is unpopular with a sleeping church. But the fire compels and constrains you to obey the call to release the warning. Jeremiah explains this fire in Jeremiah 20:7-9:

O Lord, You induced me, and I was persuaded; You are stronger than I, and have prevailed. I am in derision daily; everyone mocks me. For when I spoke, I cried out; I shouted, "Violence and plunder!" Because the word of the Lord was made to me a reproach and a derision daily. Then I said, "I will not make mention of Him, nor speak anymore in His name." But His word was in my heart like a burning fire shut up in my bones; I was weary of holding it back, and I could not.

You operate in high levels of discernment.

Discernment is part of the gift mix of the watchman. As a watchman, you may see things in the spirit that are so far away it's difficult to immediately know if what is coming is good or bad. This is where discernment comes into play. Discernment is "the quality of being able to grasp and comprehend what is obscure," also "an act of perceiving or discerning something," according to *Merriam-Webster's* dictionary. Discerning means "able to see and understand people, things, or situations clearly and intelligently."

Many watchmen are more than discerning; they operate in the gift of discerning of spirits Paul mentions in First Corinthians 12:10. The Greek word for *discerning* in that verse is *diakrino*. According to *Strong's Concordance*, it means "a distinguishing" and so "a decision" and "unto discerning good and evil." Even if you don't have the gift of discerning of spirits, you can cultivate discernment in your heart through reading the word and prayer. We see how discernment plays a strategic role in the watchman's ministry in Second Samuel 18. After Absalom died, Joab sent a messenger to give David the news. A second messenger also ran with the message, which was not protocol. Read the account in Second Samuel 18:24-27:

> *Now David was sitting between the two gates. And the watchman went up to the roof over the gate, to the wall, lifted his eyes and looked, and there was a man, running alone. Then the watchman cried out and told the king. And the king said, "If he is alone, there is news in his mouth." And he came rapidly and drew near.*
>
> *Then the watchman saw another man running, and the watchman called to the gatekeeper and said, "There is another man, running alone!" And the king said, "He also brings news." So the watchman said, "I think the running of the first is like the running of Ahimaaz the son of Zadok." And the king said, "He is a good man, and comes with good news."*

Notice how the watchman discerned who the messenger was by the way he ran—even from far off. As you mature in watchman ministry—and gain experience in this role—you will be able to discern more accurately from greater distances what is coming to the gates.

You may see in the spirit.

Not all watchmen are seers, but the seer anointing may be part of the gift mix of some watchmen. What's more, God can open your spiritual eyes to see what He wants you to see for His purposes at any time He chooses. Just like all believers can prophesy according to the will of God, all believers can see in the spirit when God chooses to open their eyes.

God has not shut off the seer realm to you. You don't have to be a seer to see—and even seers can't decide to see. All believers are at God's behest when it comes to seeing in the spirit. Your part is to desire spiritual gifts and cultivate a sensitivity in your heart and a faith in your spirit to move in this gift for His glory. You can read more about the seer gift in my book *The Seer Dimensions*.

Your message is often ignored.

The watchman's ministry is not popular and his message is often ignored by the mainstream church. Just as people ignore warning signs of cancer and ignore God's warnings about practicing sin communicated in the pages of the Bible, people have historically ignored the watchman's warnings to their own demise.

God told Ezekiel, "But the house of Israel will not listen to you, because they will not listen to Me; for all the house of Israel are impudent and hard-hearted" (Ezek. 3:7). Don't be surprised if the warning is ignored. If you are the only one standing in the gap, you can count yourself obedient and there is no blood on your hands.

You keenly observe the signs of the times.

The watchman is a keen observer of the signs of the times. They have an interest and are actively watching for things that are shut up until the time of the end (see Dan. 12:4). They are paying attention for wars and rumors of wars, false prophets, false christs, famines, pestilences, and earthquakes in diverse places, which Jesus spoke about in Scripture. Matthew 24 will particularly fascinate the end-times watchman, as well as Second Timothy 2 and Second Timothy 4.

You have an understanding of seasons.

Watchmen are interested in seasons, and some may also carry an Issachar anointing. First Chronicles 12:32 speaks of "the sons of Issachar who had understanding of the times, to know what Israel ought to do." The Hebrew word for *understanding* in this verse is *yada*. According to *The KJV Old Testament Hebrew Lexicon*, it means to know, to perceive and see, find out and discern. Sounds very prophetic to me!

God anointed this tribe of Israel to see prophetically into times and seasons. God is anointing tribes of watchmen today to see into times and seasons, but He can also allow you to enter into the Issachar dimension as He wills.

You have thick skin.

If you don't, you will need it. The watchman will be rejected in his day and perhaps celebrated in his legacy. You may have heard the phrase "set your forehead like flint." We find this twice in Scripture. Ezekiel tells us:

> *Behold, I have made your face strong against their faces, and your forehead strong against their foreheads. Like adamant stone, harder than flint, I have made your forehead; do not be afraid of them, nor be dismayed at their looks, though they are a rebellious house* (Ezekiel 3:8-9).

And this was Isaiah's confession:

> *For the Lord God will help Me; therefore I will not be disgraced; therefore I have set My face like a flint, and I know that I will not be ashamed. He is near who justifies Me;*

who will contend with Me? Let us stand together. Who is My adversary? Let him come near Me. Surely the Lord God will help Me; who is he who will condemn Me? Indeed they will all grow old like a garment; the moth will eat them up (Isaiah 50:7-9).

You feel a sense of responsibility to guard and protect.

One of the words for *watchman* in the Bible is *shamar*. The Hebrew word *shamar* speaks of a watchman who is "to keep, guard, observe, give heed, have charge of, save life, wait for, retain, treasure up (in memory), to keep (within bounds), restrain, celebrate, keep (sabbath or covenant), to be on one's guard, take heed, take care, beware, abstain." Watchmen take responsibility in prayer, to some degree, for guarding those they watch.

You are attracted to accounts of watchmen in the Bible.

If you are a baseball player, you're attracted to the styles and lives of baseball players. If you are a doctor, you are attracted to case studies from doctors in your field. If you are a watchman, you will be drawn to accounts of watchmen and their ministries in the Bible, as well as modern-day watchmen. Their ministries will intrigue you and you'll learn from their challenges and successes and the posture of their heart.

You will be determined to see what God is showing you.

A watchman doesn't just live everyday life and wait for God to interrupt him with a warning. Watchmen are determined to see, and they posture their hearts in prayer to that end. Habakkuk 2:1 demonstrates the way of the watchman: "I will stand my watch and set myself on the rampart, and watch to see what He will say to me." The New Living Translation puts it this way: "I will climb up to my watchtower and stand at my guardpost. There I will wait to see what the Lord says." Notice the effort here. The watchman will climb. The watchman will stand. The watchman will wait. The watchman will see and hear.

You will have a righteous indignation over sin and injustice.

A watchman will be more than grieved over sin and injustice; he will carry a righteous indignation over what offends God. He will love what God loves and hate what God hates. We see this in Ezekiel's life: "So the Spirit lifted me up and took me away, and I went in bitterness and in the anger of my spirit, with the strong hand of the Lord upon me" (Ezek. 3:14 BSB).

You will carry a strong fear of the Lord over your assignment.

True watchmen will carry and release the warning with a fear of the Lord. God told Ezekiel if he didn't release the warning, the blood of those who died because of his failure to sound an alarm would be on his hands. Where there is a true assignment and acceptance of this call, there will be a reverential fear of the Lord related to the consequences of failing to perform the God-ordained duty.

Chapter 3

THE ROLE OF A WATCHMAN

WHEN God makes a watchman, He makes him with the spiritual attributes, gifts, and skill sets to stand effectively in his particular role. While the watchman can shift roles or assignments according to the will of the Lord, there are baseline operations of a watchman just as there are baseline operations of a prophet.

Understanding your role or function as a watchman is vital to the success of your God-ordained mission. If you don't comprehend your watchman task in God's Kingdom, you may fail to operate in His ways, His timing—or fail to operate at all. When you understand your role, or function, in the Body of Christ, you can stand confidently in your calling and make the impact God designed.

You can find the watchman's functions in the Hebrew words for *watchman*. Biblically speaking, there are several Hebrew words for *watchman*. What you'll notice in these descriptions is that no two watchmen are exactly alike. There are specialties within the watchman world just as there are specialties in the medical field or legal arena. So there are common operations but also distinct duties that come with an individual watchman's call.

FOUR TYPES OF WATCHMAN

There are four categories of watchman, and, of course, these categories overlap. But the Lord would not have used four different words for watchman in Scripture if there were not subtleties worth noting. Just as there are different types of singers or different types of preachers, there are unique expressions of the watchman anointing.

One Hebrew word for watchman is *tsaphah*. It means "to look out or about, spy, keep watch, observe, or watch," according to *The KJV Old Testament Hebrew Lexicon*. When Eli the priest was watching, with his heart trembling, for the return of the ark of God in First Samuel 4:13, this is *tsaphah*. When watchmen stood at the tower in Jezreel spying out Jehu as he came in the glory of God in Second Kings 9:17, this was *tsaphah*. Several Scriptures that use the word *tsaphah* speak of the Lord Himself watching, including Proverbs 15:3, "The eyes of the Lord are in every place, keeping watch on the evil and the good."

In Isaiah 21:5-6,8, we also see the *tsaphah* watchman:

> *Prepare the table, set a watchman in the tower, eat and drink. Arise, you princes, anoint the shield! For thus has the Lord said to me: "Go, set a watchman, let him declare what he sees." ...Then he cried, "A lion, my Lord! I stand continually on the watchtower in the daytime; I have sat at my post every night."*

Another Hebrew expression of watchman is *natsar*. This is a type of watchman that includes a stronger thrust to guard. According to *The KJV Old Testament Hebrew Lexicon*, *natsar* means "to guard, watch, watch over, keep" and "to preserve, guard from dangers, to keep, observe, guard with fidelity, to keep secret, to be kept close, be blockaded." This is also the type of watchman who calls the church to worship the Lord in unity. Jeremiah 31:6 reads, "The day will come when watchmen will shout from the hill country of Ephraim, 'Come, let us go up to Jerusalem to worship the Lord our God'" (NLT).

Shamar has become a popular expression of the watchman with some modern-day teachers, even though this was not the word used to describe Ezekiel's function. The Hebrew word *shamar* speaks of a watchman who is "to keep, guard, observe, give heed, have charge of, save life, wait for, retain, treasure up (in memory), to keep (within bounds), restrain, celebrate, keep (sabbath or covenant), to be on one's guard, take heed, take care, beware, abstain." The *shamar* watchman is one who watches daily at God's gates (see Prov. 8:34). According to *The International Standard Bible Encyclopedia*:

> The distinction in meaning between the various words is clear, tsopheh having the idea of "outlooker" and notser that of "careful watcher" (being applied even to besiegers from outside: Jeremiah 4:16, "watchers"), while shomer also embraces the idea of "defending" or "guarding." In Isaiah 21:6 metsappeh [*tsaphah*] is to be taken generally in the sense of "watch."

The watchman's role, in a nutshell, is to keep watch, spy out the enemy's plans, look for the coming of the Lord, discern the work of angels, and generally be on guard. The watchman gives warning, blows trumpets, sounds the alarm, stands in the gap, and makes up the hedge. The watchman's role is one of the heaviest responsibilities in the Bible and the only time the Lord tells us the blood will be on our hands if we fail to obey the call to warn.

Now, lest the enemy bring you into condemnation—there is no condemnation in Christ Jesus (Rom. 8:1)—I understand and there have been times when I didn't have a way to warn anyone. If that happens, you sound the alarm in intercession. Cry out to the Lord in prayer to push back the darkness or to intercede for the people group He's highlighting. The idea is just to take action on what God shows you. Let's break this down further:

WATCHING FOR MOVEMENT IN THE SPIRIT

The watchman is charged with being spiritually aware, watching, and listening for any signs of movement in the spirit. Many times, it's enemy operations for which we're looking. First Peter 5:8 says, "Be well balanced (temperate, sober of mind), be vigilant and cautious at all times; for that enemy of yours, the devil, roams around like a lion roaring [in fierce hunger], seeking someone to seize upon and devour" (AMPC).

We absolutely must be on the lookout for devils on the loose. But as watchmen, we have to be careful not to get hyper-focused on the enemy. We also have to look and listen for the Lord. God told Ezekiel, "Give them warning from Me." That means at times we're watching for the Lord warning us not of demon powers, but of the sin that allows demon powers to enter—the sin that eats away at our hedge of protection.

At other times, we're watching for angels or the King of Glory Himself approaching so we don't miss the day of our visitation. Unbalanced watchmen can trip over their own discernment. Remember, if you're seeing demonic activity in the spirit, the Lord is in there somewhere because God is everywhere.

Remember Amos 3:7: "Surely the Lord God does nothing, unless He reveals His secret to His servants the prophets." Not all watchmen are prophets, but watchmen are standing in a prophetic function to see and hear in the spirit realm. God might not show you everything, but He will show you what you need to see to serve His Kingdom in your realm of authority. We shouldn't be blindsided by terror attacks in our city, for example. As watchmen, we should see the danger in the spirit and take action.

GUARD YOUR SPHERE OF INFLUENCE

Watchmen tend to be assigned to specific people groups, whether it's the church or to a specific nation, such as Israel. Likely, you aren't called to warn everybody, but the watchman is called to warn somebody. Your assignment may be to your family, your local church, the Body of Christ, a denomination, etc. You can discern your calling by locating your passion and taking note to whom your warnings are directed.

The prophet said, "I will stand my watch and set myself on the rampart, and watch to see what He will say to me, and what I will answer when I am corrected" (Hab. 2:1). Watchmen have a watch. They have a territory or spheres of influence for which they are responsible. Some watchmen are primarily called to watch in the government; others are called to the church or the entertainment industry.

Watchmen will have a grace for the place they are called to watch. But the modern watchman must also press in to be versatile or ambidextrous in the spirit. If you primarily hear, you need to press in to see. If you primarily see, you need to stretch yourself to hear in greater detail the strategy the Lord wants to share. Proverbs 20:12 says, "The hearing ear and the seeing eye, the Lord has made them both." I believe God wants to cause eyes to hear and ears to see in this season, prophetically speaking.

Scripture reveals three types of prophetic sentinels whose mission is to stand guard, keep watch, and report what they see. We find Old Testament prophets on the walls, walking in the streets of the city, and in the countryside.

"I have set watchmen on your walls, O Jerusalem; they shall never hold their peace day or night. You who make mention of the Lord, do not keep not silent" (Isa. 62:6). Watchmen on the walls are positioned to see far distances in the spirit and discern whether friend or foe is approaching. The watchman gives word to those in authority so they can decide whether to sound an alarm of welcome or an alarm of war. In today's local church, these watchmen help protect against enemy attacks. Every prophet is called to this post.

"'They surround Jerusalem like watchmen around a field, for my people have rebelled against me,' says the Lord" (Jer. 4:17 NLT). This relates to the watchmen in the harvest fields. Watchmen have a clear role in evangelism as watchmen who protect gospel-preaching efforts against the destructive work of principalities and powers that keep the lost from hearing the truth. Watchmen should be deployed on local church outreaches and international missions to watch, guard, pull down, and destroy opposition to the Good News. "The watchmen found me as they made their rounds in the city" (Song of Sol. 3:3; 5:7 NIV). In today's times, this watchman is assigned to stand guard over the Body of Christ to see emerging problems. This is a larger responsibility that carries with it a heavier prayer burden and greater implications for the church at large.

DISCERN THE DIFFERENCE BETWEEN FRIEND AND FOE

The watchman is charged with discerning between friend and foe—or even between demon and demon. If you call it God and it's the enemy, the people will be unprepared for the onslaught. If you call it the enemy and it's God, people may resist the Lord's work. If you call it Jezebel and it's Leviathan, you'll be fighting the wrong enemy. Consider Second Kings 9:17-20:

> *Now a watchman stood on the tower in Jezreel, and he saw the company of Jehu as he came, and said, "I see a company of men." And Joram said, "Get a horseman and send him to meet them, and let him say, 'Is it peace?'" So the horseman went to meet him, and said, "Thus says the king: 'Is it peace?'" And Jehu said, "What have you to do with peace? Turn around and follow me." So the watchman reported, saying, "The messenger went to them, but is not coming back." Then he sent out a second horseman who came to them, and said, "Thus says the king: 'Is it peace?'" And Jehu answered, "What have you to do with peace? Turn around and follow me." So the watchman reported, saying, "He went up to them and is not coming back; and the driving is like the driving of Jehu the son of Nimshi, for he drives furiously!"*

The watchman was able to distinguish who was riding because he was familiar with the characters. This is why you need to be familiar with the ways of the Lord and the ways of the enemy. The Lord runs differently than the enemy, but the enemy can try to mimic the running of the Lord.

WARN THE CHURCH

I have set watchmen on your walls, O Jerusalem; they shall never hold their peace day or night. You who make mention of the Lord, do not keep silent (Isaiah 62:6).

Where was Isaiah set? On the walls of Jerusalem. In today's vernacular, that translates to the Body of Christ at large—the church. Remember, God told Ezekiel, "Son of man, I have made you a watchman for the house of Israel" (Ezek. 3:17).

Beyond the fact that there is a making process for the watchman, which includes understanding the truths from the Word of God presented in this book, we have to understand the watchman's role is primarily to the church. God called watchmen to warn His people primarily, though Jonah did travel to Nineveh to warn the people of that city of destruction. As a watchman, we have to share God's warning even if we don't like it or we could end up in the belly of a whale—like Jonah.

God told Ezekiel, "Son of man, I have made you a watchman for the house of Israel; therefore hear a word from My mouth, and give them warning from Me" (Ezek. 3:17). That doesn't leave the watchman any wiggle room. It's not personal preference. The watchman doesn't really have a choice.

Not to release the warning—or making intercession—is sheer disobedience. No true believer wants to be disobedient to God. If you have missed it, ask the Lord's forgiveness and move on. From then on, stay in obedience to pray when God shows you something that you are sure is from God. The Lord never just shows one person when it is an extremely critical situation. However, you need to grow in being a watchman.

And remember, when sharing that message it needs to be clear what part is the Lord speaking and what part is your analysis or opinion or takeaway. The watchman must never present his opinions as the word of the Lord.

What are we warning the church of? Not just demons, but sin and false teachings. Ezekiel primarily warned the church of sin. Sin in the church today looks much different than sin in the church of Ezekiel's day—or at least they are expressed differently or are more widely accepted. Widespread abortion, homosexuality, obscene wealth while extreme poverty exists, racism, and other isms that exist inside the church grieve the Lord, and few want to address it.

Modern-day watchmen are charged with warning of false teachings, which is not new because Paul the apostle warned of Gnosticism and other errors trying to infiltrate the early church. In his book *Spiritual Avalanche*, the late Steve Hill warned of seven great lies in the church today. He lists those as 1) an overemphasis on prosperity; 2) exaggerated views of grace; 3) antinomianism, which literally means "against law"; 4) deification of man; 5) challenging the authority of the Word; 6) rejecting hell; and 7) universal reconciliation. This warning was the last major trumpet blow Hill released before he died of cancer in 2014.

REPORT TO THOSE IN AUTHORITY

Now David was sitting between the two gates. And the watchman went up to the roof over the gate, to the wall, lifted his eyes and looked, and there was a man, running alone. Then the watchman cried out and told the king. And

the king said, "If he is alone, there is news in his mouth."
And he came rapidly and drew near (2 Samuel 18:24-25).

If you are a watchman in the church, you need to report what you see (at the right time and in the right way) to those in authority so they can decide what to do with the warning. That doesn't prevent you from praying, but you must submit your gift to the authority of your church.

If you are not in a church and receive a serious warning for the Body of Christ that may scare people, you need to submit that to someone of higher rank in the spirit than you to judge. A watchman under authority is a powerful weapon in the Kingdom of God.

WORK WITH THE GATEKEEPERS

Watchmen and gatekeepers must work hand in hand. A gatekeeper is one who guards the gate or one who controls access. The gatekeeper is an intercessor who makes a wall. Their job is to forbid access to unauthorized persons and demonic intruders. The watchman warns the gatekeeper who is coming, whether friend of foe. The gatekeeper is not stationed in a watchtower to see far distances. The gatekeeper works on the ground.

Second Samuel 18:25-26 explains this dynamic:

> *Then the watchman cried out and told the king. And the king said, "If he is alone, there is news in his mouth." And he came rapidly and drew near. Then the watchman saw another man running, and the watchman called to the gatekeeper and said, "There is another man, running alone!"*

MAKE INTERCESSION

Many feel the watchman's job is over when he sounds the alarm. But the watchman's job is just beginning. It's not difficult to see what the enemy is doing. The harder portion of the job is to stand in the gap and make up the hedge—and gather others to do so in urgency until the enemy is shut out or the opposition to the Lord's entrance is dealt with in the spirit.

Chapter 4

THE WARNING MINISTRY

WHEN *Charisma* magazine asked me to start a column on its Charisma News online property, it didn't take me long to determine a theme: "Watchman on the Wall." During that season, I was heavy into reporting on the culture wars, which is one aspect of the watchman's ministry. Over the years, God stationed me more prophetically to warn about as many spiritual dangers as natural dangers and cultural dangers.

See, a watchman can warn about sin—which is the assignment of a culture-war watchman. Dr. Michael Brown is a modern-day example of the culture-war watchman, dissecting with boldness and grace the issues in a post-modern world that are infiltrating the church. Some watchmen are assigned to the church, to warn of sin and spirits that overtake Christians. Still others warn about natural disasters, plagues, and the end times.

Every watchman has a station, and, of course, there can be crossover assignments—and God can shift you into new roles in new seasons. I've stood as a watchman in many different operations, but my primary function is warning about spirits attacking the church. Regardless of the watchman's expertise or assignment, the common denominators in the watchman's ministry are warning and intercession.

Warn means "to give notice to beforehand especially of danger or evil; to give admonishing advice to: counsel; to call to one's attention: inform," according to *Merriam-Webster*'s dictionary. Warning is addressing, alerting, cautioning, notifying, preparing, summoning, urging, exhorting, reproving, directing, reminding, prompting and advocating.

When God told Ezekiel to give the people a warning for Him in Ezekiel 3:17, the Hebrew word for *warning* in that verse is *zahar*. According to *The KVJ Old Testament Hebrew Lexicon*, it means "to admonish, warn, teach, shine, send out light, be light, be shining."

These references to shining remind me of the ministry of John the Baptist, to whom I have related since I was called into ministry. When Jesus spoke of John, He revealed his role as a watchman prophet whose warnings of the coming Messiah were largely ignored in his day:

> *Yet I do not receive testimony from man, but I say these things that you may be saved. He was the burning and shining lamp, and you were willing for a time to rejoice in his light. But I have a greater witness than John's; for the works which the Father has given Me to finish—the very works that I do—bear witness of Me, that the Father has sent Me* (John 5:34-36).

A JOHN THE BAPTIST MANTLE

God called me into prophetic ministry in a church. An apostle prayed over me and prophesied, "I've called you to be a voice of governing authority. I release that voice." I had no idea what that meant. I was a brand-new Christian. I went home and started studying what the Bible said about governing and the voice. I was still largely clueless, but determined. I closed my Bible and asked God what He meant, and was led to open my Bible again.

When I opened the Bible, it landed on Matthew 3:3:

> *For this is he who was spoken of by the prophet Isaiah, saying: "The voice of one crying in the wilderness: 'Prepare the way of the Lord; Make His paths straight.'"*

Of course, this Scripture is speaking of John the Baptist. My spirit leaped, though I still did not understand what God was saying. Randomly, I flipped the pages. I landed on Mark 1:3, which essentially said the same thing. Now God had my attention. I flipped the pages again and landed on John 1:23, which repeated the same Scripture.

Even though I was a young Christian, I understood that something about my ministry would be like John the Baptist's. John didn't perform any mighty miracles that we know of. He didn't heal the sick, raise the dead, cleanse the lepers, or cast out demons that we know of. John the Baptist had a warning ministry of which we are all well aware. He was a powerful preacher with a heart-turning ministry like Elijah's. He burned and shone, though few wanted to hear what he had to say.

John's main warning: "Repent, for the kingdom of heaven is at hand!" (Matt. 3:2). This sounds somewhat like Ezekiel's prophetic warning: "Repent, and turn from all your transgressions, so that iniquity will not be your ruin" (Ezek. 18:30). John was faithful to preach day in and day out a message that warned the Messiah was soon to come. In Matthew 3:9-11 we read:

> *And do not think to say to yourselves, "We have Abraham as our father." For I say to you that God is able to raise up*

children to Abraham from these stones. And even now the
ax is laid to the root of the trees. Therefore every tree which
does not bear good fruit is cut down and thrown into the
fire. I indeed baptize you with water unto repentance, but
He who is coming after me is mightier than I, whose san-
dals I am not worthy to carry. He will baptize you with the
Holy Spirit and fire.

John's call almost seems evangelistic, like unto a Billy Graham. John was preparing the way for the First Coming of the Messiah. Billy Graham was known to preach fire and brimstone messages—also called "turn or burn" sermons. In fact, in Graham's last book, *Where I Am: Heaven, Eternity, and Our Life Beyond*, he offers one of his last warnings:

Hell is a place of sorrow and unrest, a place of wailing and a furnace of fire.... And it is where many will spend eternity. If you accept any part of the Bible, you are forced to accept the reality of hell, the place for punishment for those who reject Christ.[1]

MODERN-DAY JOHN THE BAPTISTS RISING

I believe modern-day John the Baptists are rising as we approach the Second Coming of the Lord. Remember John's calling, which Isaiah—another watchman—prophesied:

The voice of one crying in the wilderness: "Prepare the way
of the Lord; make straight in the desert a highway for our
God. Every valley shall be exalted and every mountain and

hill brought low; the crooked places shall be made straight and the rough places smooth; the glory of the Lord shall be revealed, and all flesh shall see it together; for the mouth of the Lord has spoken" (Isaiah 40:3-5).

A John the Baptist watchman isn't always evangelistic, but is a person of self-denial. He took a Nazirite vow and lived in the wilderness most of his life and ate no delicacies. In fact, his food was locusts and wild honey (see Matt. 3:4). You might say John lived a fasted lifestyle. He was truly in the world but not of the world (see John 17:16). John possessed courage to speak hard words. He confronted both political and religious leaders in his day, warning them of the consequences of their sin—and ultimately lost his head because of it.

A John the Baptist watchman is obedient to share warnings that may bring persecution and walks in humility. He wants to draw people to Christ rather than himself. In fact, when John's disciples started following Jesus he did not take exception to the hit on his ministry. Instead, he explained, "He must increase, but I must decrease. He who comes from above is above all; he who is of the earth is earthly and speaks of the earth. He who comes from heaven is above all" (John 3:30-31).

John the Baptist was zealous to warn, burning and shining for the Lord. Those were Jesus' words in John 5:35: "He was the burning and shining lamp, and you were willing for a time to rejoice in his light." The Greek word for *burn* in that verse is *kaio*, which means "to set on fire." John the Baptist is a prime example of what it means to be on fire for God. He was faithful to complete his mission to warn.

POPULAR WITH MAN OR GOD?

I've taken on a John the Baptist-like mantle. It hasn't made me popular with man, but I know it has been pleasing to heaven. Watchmen must take a Galatians 1:10 attitude: "For do I now persuade men, or God? Or do I seek to please men? For if I still pleased men, I would not be a bond-servant of Christ."

A watchman is a bondservant of Christ in the same way an apostle or prophet is. In reality, all Christians are servants to do Christ's bidding. The watchman, though, will have blood on his hands if he doesn't complete the mission. We must seek to please God, who examines our hearts (see 1 Thess. 2:4).

I have over the years issued hard-hitting warnings on many fronts, but much of it is released to the church itself. In 2016, the Lord showed me clearly a spirit rising that's causing these unreasonable offenses. It was and still is satan's plot to divide believers in an hour of church history when it's more vital than perhaps ever before that we unite on our common beliefs. When I asked the Lord about this, He explained what is going on:

> A spirit of offense is rising and running rampant through the church. Those who are easily offended are candidates for the Great Falling Away. Those who cultivate and maintain an unoffendable heart will escape many of the assignments the enemy will launch in the days to come.
>
> For My people must band together in this hour and refuse to allow petty arguments and soulish imaginations separate them. This is the time to press into community

and relationship and reject the demonic notions and wisdom the enemy is pouring out.

The love of many is waxing cold. Brother is turning against brother and sister against sister—in My body. You must come to the unity of the faith in order to accomplish what I've called you to do in this hour. The time is upon you. The opportunity is before you. Lay aside the resentment, bitterness, and unforgiveness and, as far as it depends upon you, seek peace with all men.

Humble yourselves even among those who you feel are your enemies, and I will work to bring reconciliation that sets the scene for unity from which the anointing flows. You need My anointing to combat the antichrist spirits rising in this hour.

Many of My people are wrestling in their flesh, engaging in works of the flesh, and otherwise letting the flesh lead in battle—and they are battling flesh instead of the spirits influencing the flesh. This is the result of offense. Forgive, let go, embrace your brothers and sisters despite their flaws and sins. I have.

I warned the body and, of course, some were offended. I've learned one of the quickest ways to offend a Christian is to suggest they are offended. But this is a sign of the times. Like John the Baptist warned of the greatest sign of his times—the sign of the first coming of the Messiah—God has me warning about end-times signs. Jesus said plainly that in the end times, "And then many will be offended, will betray one another, and will hate one another. Then many false prophets will rise up and deceive many" (Matt. 24:10-11).

That brings me to the primary thrust of my warning ministry. It seems the common denominator or running theme in my ministry is warning of false spirits, particularly false prophets and teachers. My book *Discerning Prophetic Witchcraft* is the culmination of over twenty years of steady warnings about false spirits and false prophets. I've consistently and loudly warned the Body of Christ and taught them how to discern spirits, judge prophecy, and otherwise study to show themselves approved.

I've warned about the witch movement appearing with Christian witches rising in the name of Jesus. I've warned about secular humanist agendas, atheistic agendas, religious agendas, and many other agendas through the years. Of course, that's not the extent of my warning ministry. God has diversified me over the years—and He will likely diversify your warning ministry as well.

YOU ARE RESPONSIBLE TO WARN

The warning ministry is not relegated to prophets and watchmen only. Every believer has the ability to stand, watch, warn, and pray. When I was young in the Lord, I was troubled because I had so many warnings and I couldn't see how that fit into the gift of prophecy. We were taught that prophecy should edify, comfort, and exhort, according to First Corinthians 14:3. I asked an elder prophet about this and he helped me understand that the warning aspect is included in exhortation.

While the dictionary definition of *exhortation* is "language intended to incite or encourage," the Bible definition gives more clarity. The Greek word for *exhortation* in First Corinthians 14:3 is *paraklesis*. According to *The KJV New Testament Greek Lexicon*, in the context of the watchman it means a calling near, summons, admonition, persuasive discourse, stirring address, instructive, and admonitory. That sounds like a warning to me.

As a watchman, it's not enough to see what's coming down the pike. If you don't warn the people, God says the blood will be on your hands. What does that mean, really? The New Living Translation puts it this way, "I will hold you responsible for their deaths" (Ezek. 3:18). The Message says, "I'll hold you responsible." *Pulpit Commentary* writes:

> But the unfaithful watchman has his responsibility. It is as though the blood of the sinner had been shed. His guilt may be described in the same words as that of Cain (Gen. 9:5). Compare St. Paul's words in Acts 18:6 and Acts 20:26 as echoes of Ezekiel's thought.

Let's take *Pulpit Commentary's* suggestion and look at these Scriptures. Genesis 9:5 reads, "Surely for your lifeblood I will demand a reckoning; from the hand of every beast I will require it, and from the hand of man. From the hand of every man's brother I will require the life of man." And Paul said in Acts 20:25-26, "And indeed, now I know that you all, among whom I have gone preaching the kingdom of God, will see my face no more. Therefore I testify to you this day that I am innocent of the blood of all men."

Now you can see why the spirit of the fear of the Lord came upon me in the middle of the night while lying on that bunk bed in Nicaragua. This is not a game or a joke. This is a serious responsibility. In this sense, we are our brother's keeper. Although people are not completely exempt from the consequences of danger or sin because the watchman failed to warn, the watchman is held responsible.

GIVE THEM WARNING FOR ME

Watching is an aspect of the Lord's character—and so is warning. The Lord sees everything and He has given us His word to warn us of the consequences of sin. The Holy Spirit is the informant behind the watchman's ministry. The Holy Spirit, in other words, is the one who gives prophetic intelligence to the watchman so the watchman can, in turn, warn the people. Remember, God told Ezekiel in Ezekiel 3:17-19:

> *Son of man, I have made you a watchman for the house of Israel; therefore hear a word from My mouth, and give them warning from Me: When I say to the wicked, "You shall surely die," and you give him no warning, nor speak to warn the wicked from his wicked way, to save his life, that same wicked man shall die in his iniquity; but his blood I will require at your hand. Yet, if you warn the wicked, and he does not turn from his wickedness, nor from his wicked way, he shall die in his iniquity; but you have delivered your soul.*

Notice the words "give them warning from Me." The watchman is only voicing the warning. The warning comes from the Lord. God has set up watchmen to warn since the days of Exodus. The Lord told Moses to warn the Israelites: "Go down and warn the people, lest they break through to gaze at the Lord, and many of them perish. Also let the priests who come near the Lord consecrate themselves, lest the Lord break out against them" (Exod. 19:21-22). The Lord is always faithful to warn His people. The question is whether the watchman is awake and paying attention and willing to release the warning despite potential persecution.

When Jesus walked the earth, fully God and fully man, He offered many warnings. Jesus warned us about sin, hypocritical religious leaders, false prophets, false christs, the devil, hell, being judgmental, and the destruction of Jerusalem. Jesus warned about the great tribulation and to be ready for His Second Coming. Jesus warned about the signs of the times and the end of the age. Matthew 24 is full of warnings from beginning to end. And in Matthew 24:36-44, He warns:

> *But of that day and hour no one knows, not even the angels of heaven, but My Father only. But as the days of Noah were, so also will the coming of the Son of Man be. For as in the days before the flood, they were eating and drinking, marrying and giving in marriage, until the day that Noah entered the ark, and did not know until the flood came and took them all away, so also will the coming of the Son of Man be.*
>
> *Then two men will be in the field: one will be taken and the other left. Two women will be grinding at the mill: one will be taken and the other left. Watch therefore, for you do not know what hour your Lord is coming. But know this, that if the master of the house had known what hour the thief would come, he would have watched and not allowed his house to be broken into. Therefore you also be ready, for the Son of Man is coming at an hour you do not expect.*

A CRITICAL WARNING TO WATCHMEN

Prophetically speaking, there's never been a more critical time for the watchman to take the warning aspect of his ministry seriously. It's not enough for you to know a thing. You need to warn about a thing. You have to take the Ezekiel 3 and 33 verses about the blood on your hands seriously, because it is serious. Your warnings—or your intercession in your prayer closet—could help avert disaster, cause a person to be protected from an attack of Satan, or even help stop a terrorist attack! *Many are falling away or passing away because the watchmen are jostling for first place in a social media popularity contest.*

Let the spirit of the fear of the Lord rest upon you. This ministry is not designed for you to gain a large following of believers who sing your praise. Consider the ministry of the watchman in the Bible. He was largely hated, despised, often persecuted. Jeremiah wasn't called the weeping prophet for nothing. He didn't write the Book of Lamentations because he was on a joy ride. While we can have joy and peace standing as a watchman for God's glory, we must accept that we may be ignored and even hated. Jesus said:

> *If the world hates you, you know that it hated Me before it hated you. If you were of the world, the world would love its own. Yet because you are not of the world, but I chose you out of the world, therefore the world hates you. Remember the word that I said to you, "A servant is not greater than his master." If they persecuted Me, they will also persecute you. If they kept My word, they will keep yours also* (John 15:18-20).

This is a word to all believers—how much more so of watchmen?

DEVELOP A THICK SKIN

You have to develop thick skin to stand in this office—or even to warn your inner circle of friends and family. I am grateful the Lord prepared me to set my forehead like flint as a journalist. In the media world, I got a lot of rejection letters before I was successful. I received a lot of red ink on my stories from elder editors before I grew into the writer I am now. I got smacked with many nasty comments that used to rattle me before I learned to let it roll off my back.

I am more concerned with what God wants me to say than what other people say about me. Take on this mindset and it will shield you from the impact of the persecution. And remember this charge in Ezekiel 3:17-21:

> *Son of man, I have made you a watchman for the house of Israel; therefore hear a word from My mouth, and give them warning from Me: When I say to the wicked, "You shall surely die," and you give him no warning, nor speak to warn the wicked from his wicked way, to save his life, that same wicked man shall die in his iniquity; but his blood I will require at your hand. Yet, if you warn the wicked, and he does not turn from his wickedness, nor from his wicked way, he shall die in his iniquity; but you have delivered your soul.*
>
> *Again, when a righteous man turns from his righteousness and commits iniquity, and I lay a stumbling block before him, he shall die; because you did not give him warning, he shall die in his sin, and his righteousness which he has done shall not be remembered; but his blood I will require at your hand. Nevertheless if you warn the righteous man that the righteous should not sin, and he does not sin, he shall surely live because he took warning; also you will have delivered your soul.*

Forerunner Commentary writes:

Obviously, such a job would bring him into conflict with the people; people do not like to hear such a message. They do not like to hear that things are going down the tubes, and especially that they are personally responsible. But that is basically what the watchman's message is. Nothing changes unless it begins in the individual. The individual must change! He must repent and go God's way. As more individuals do this, society will change. However, Ezekiel has already been told that everything he says will fall on deaf ears, so he must have a forehead of flint, an undaunted, courageous spirit, to keep repeating the message until he dies.

This is your charge, watchman.

NOTE

1. Billy Graham, *Where I Am: Heaven, Eternity, and Our Life Beyond* (Nashville, TN: Thomas Nelson, 2015), 202-203.

Chapter 5

CULTIVATING A WATCHMAN'S EYE

OST of us know how to pray. Fewer understand the mechanics of watching in the spirit. This is part of the making of a watchman. The reality is if you don't see and hear accurately it's more difficult to pray accurately for God's will to be done in any given situation. If you don't see the enemy coming—or if you don't see the glory of the Lord coming—how can you pray accordingly?

With this understanding, then, our great quest is to cultivate a watchman's eye. A watchman's eye is one that sees what the Lord wants him to see. Oftentimes, the watching is done in prayer. But as you advance in the watchman's ministry, you will begin to have spiritual insight into what the enemy is doing outside your times of dedicated prayer. In other words, if you cultivate your watchman's eye, you will discern spiritual activity while walking through everyday life.

Habakkuk was a prophet who cultivated a watchman's eye. His recorded example in Habakkuk 2 gives us some immediate clues how to develop the skills we need to watch, as well as how the Lord responds to the persevering watchman. Habakkuk 2:1-3 reads:

I will stand my watch and set myself on the rampart, and watch to see what He will say to me, and what I will answer when I am corrected. Then the Lord answered me and said: "Write the vision and make it plain on tablets, that he may run who reads it. For the vision is yet for an appointed time; but at the end it will speak, and it will not lie. Though it tarries, wait for it; because it will surely come, it will not tarry."

Habakkuk was dedicated to watching, waiting, seeing, listening, and obeying. Make no mistake, it's work to watch. Notice that God answered his watching. He was standing and watching. He wasn't praying. Yet God answered his watching. In some ways, the watching itself is a silent prayer for revelation about what is happening in the spiritual realm.

It takes patience to watch. It takes both natural and spiritual discipline to watch. It takes an enduring spirit to watch. So, then, cultivating a watchman's eye isn't all about seeing. There's more to it than that—much more. We can learn plenty about cultivating a watchman's eye from these verses.

CLIMBING HIGHER TO SEE

The New Living Translation of Habakkuk 2:1 reads, "I will climb up to my watchtower and stand at my guardpost. There I will wait to see what the Lord says and how he will answer my complaint." Notice how Habakkuk had to take action—he had to climb. Habakkuk had to position himself to gain the right perspective on the landscape, and that meant ascending to a height that offered a different vantage point.

When I was in Scotland, I climbed up to the top of the National Wallace Monument in Stirling. The tower stands on the shoulder of the Abbey Craig, a hilltop overlooking the city. I climbed every single one of the 246 steps on the spiral staircase to get to the top. It was work. Hard work. But from atop that tower I could see with clarity things my eye never would have spied out from the bottom of the monument.

Modern-day watchmen are not physically climbing stairs to get to the top of the watchtower. But they must climb to that place of perspective through prayer. Indeed, through prayer, meditation on the Word, silence, and worship you can ascend to the top of the tower. You can climb up to your post. At times, you have to still your soul to make this spiritual climb, and that can mean entering the silent dimension. As I wrote in my book, *The Seer Dimensions*:

> Silence is the foundation of contemplative prayer. Contemplative prayer opens your eyes in ways other prayer does not because it leads you into intimacy with God, the source of all revelation. Contemplative prayer is centuries old and is actually rooted in monks, hermits and nuns. I do not agree with the doctrines of the Catholic church, but the reality is those who set themselves apart in His presence lived from the inside out.
>
> Contemplative prayer is a thoughtful practice where you focus on the Word of God to the point where you drown out other thoughts, feelings and temporal distractions. You are focusing on the Father, Son and Holy Spirit within you rather than the Father, Son and Holy Spirit outside of you. God's voice becomes more clear through this practice.

At times, repentance precedes this spiritual climbing. If you have known sin in your life, you will not see or hear clearly. In fact, you can't even climb to the place from which God is calling you to watch if you have sin on your hands. Psalm 24:3-4 reveals:

> *Who may ascend into the hill of the Lord? Or who may stand in His holy place? He who has clean hands and a pure heart, who has not lifted up his soul to an idol, nor sworn deceitfully.*

At times, God will invite the watchman to "come up here." In Revelation 4:1 we read: "After these things I looked, and behold, a door standing open in heaven. And the first voice which I heard was like a trumpet speaking with me, saying, 'Come up here, and I will show you things which must take place after this.'" This was John the Revelator's invitation to watch scenes from the end times unfold right before his very eyes.

Amos recorded these prophetic words: "Surely the Lord God does nothing, unless He reveals His secret to His servants the prophets" (Amos 3:7). All watchmen are not prophets, but I believe if God has called you to watch and you do so faithfully—be His servant, be a friend of God—He will share His secrets with you for the sake of His Kingdom.

STANDING GUARD AND SET IN PLACE

After Habakkuk climbed, he stood. Notice he was standing—not slumbering, not sitting down. He was standing. The Hebrew word for *stand* in this verse is telling. When we think of standing, we may think of standing around talking to friends or standing in line at a store. But the type of standing Habakkuk did—and the type of standing the watchman does—goes way beyond being erect on your two feet.

The Hebrew word for *stand* in this verse is *amad*. According to *The KJV Old Testament Hebrew Lexicon*, it means to remain. In other words, Habakkuk didn't climb all that way to stand atop the tower for a few minutes to enjoy the scenery until he was bored. He had a mind to stand there until he received the revelation he was looking for. He worked too hard to get there and he wasn't about to turn around and come back down without getting what he was after.

Stand also means "endure." It takes endurance to operate in the watchman anointing. Being a watchman is not like watching TV. You can't turn on the big screen and channel surf until you find something that interests you. Watchmen need endurance, sort of like bird watchers who sit in silence for hours in the hopes of spotting a bluebird.

Stand means to take one's stand, be in a standing attitude, stand still, stand upright. Standing and watching go hand in hand. In First Corinthians 16:13, Paul tells the church at Corinth: "Watch, stand fast in the faith, be brave, be strong." The watchman must learn to stand firm in the faith and stand fast in the Lord. The good news is, God is able to make you stand (see Rom. 14:4).

Habakkuk said he would *set* himself on the rampart. The Christian Standard Bible puts it this way: "station myself on the lookout tower." The Hebrew word for *set* in this verse is *yatsab*. According to *The KJV Old Testament Hebrew Lexicon*, it means "to place, set, stand, set or station, present oneself." The watchman must present himself before the Lord, ready to watch.

WAIT AND SEE

Habakkuk said he would "watch to see." The New International Version says, "I will look to see." The English Standard Version says "look out to see." The New Living Translation says "I will wait to see." The watchman must be an expert not only at watching, but waiting. In Bible days, watchmen could watch days or weeks at a time and not see much of significance, but they were faithful to stand on their post regardless. See, it's not always about seeing something. Seeing nothing can be a good thing. If the coast is clear, that means the land is at peace.

Psalm 130:5-6, "I wait for the Lord, with bated breath I wait; I long for His Word! My soul waits for the Lord, more than watchmen for the morning, more than watchmen for the morning" (MEV). You can't separate the watchman from waiting. The two go hand in hand. Newly minted watchmen may be uncomfortable in this process and be tempted to fall asleep at their watch. But if we want to cultivate a watchman's eye—if we want gain the Lord's perspective—we need to be willing to wait until He shows us something.

Keep Isaiah 40:31 in mind:

> *But those who wait for the Lord [who expect, look for, and hope in Him] shall change and renew their strength and power; they shall lift their wings and mount up [close to God] as eagles [mount up to the sun]; they shall run and not be weary, they shall walk and not faint or become tired* (AMPC).

We have to keep looking, and many times that means we have to keep waiting. We can only see what He shows us. When we do wait, we mount up with wings like eagles. In other words, we gain God's perspective.

Psalm 37:7 gives us a secret to successful waiting: "Be still before the Lord and wait patiently for Him" (ESV). If you are going to cultivate a watchman's eye, you have to set aside the multi-tasking and the mind traffic and be still. Understand that the Hebrew word for *wait* is not a passive, boring waiting that tempts you to sleep and slumber. No, the Hebrew word for *wait* is *qavah*. It is an active word that means to "look for," according to *The KJV Old Testament Hebrew Lexicon*. Have you ever been waiting for a friend in the airport? It's crowded. You are waiting, but you are actively looking while you wait.

Qavah means to expect. When the watchman waits, he's expecting to see. That expectation breeds an alert eye. *Qavah* means to look eagerly for, to lie in wait for, or to linger for. Can you see the action in these definitions? The watchman is looking for action in the spirit. Sometimes things happen so fast, if you aren't waiting, expecting, and looking for it, you'll miss it.

Have you ever been watching a basketball game and looked down at your phone and missed what the announcers are saying was one of the greatest slam dunks of all time? Your friends are cheering and you're like, "What happened?" Thankfully, there are replays of sporting events. In the spirit, there's no guarantee of a replay. The watchman must wait.

I liken watching to praying with your eyes. It's like your eyes crying out to God to show you what He wants you to see and demonstrating your faith for a prayer answer by continuing to look.

CLEAN HANDS, PURE HEART

The watchman's eyes and heart are connected. If your heart is not pure, your spiritual eyes can grow dim. Remember, watchmen climbed up to the top of the tower to get the best possible view. Spiritually, that correlates with ascending the hill of the Lord. Not everybody, not even if they have a watchman's anointing, is granted access to this viewpoint.

Psalm 24:3-4 offers insight: "Who may ascend into the hill of the Lord? Or who may stand in His holy place? He who has clean hands and a pure heart, who has not lifted up his soul to an idol, nor sworn deceitfully." This is talking about entering the presence of the Lord, which is the best place from which to watch. But it also gives qualifications.

Clean hands are found on someone "whose actions and conversation are holy and unblameable," according to *Benson Commentary*. No watchman is perfect, but we should strive for one hundredfold obedience to the Lord. That must be our heart posture.

A pure heart, Benson writes, is one "purged from hypocrisy, and corrupt desires and designs, and careful to approve itself to God, as well as men, ordering a man's very thoughts, intentions, and affections, according to God's Word. This is fitly added, because a man may keep his hands clean, in a good measure, from mere worldly motives, and without any respect to God, and even with an evil design." In other words, the watchman can have clean hands without a pure heart in terms of loving God.

BEWARE BLINDING IDOLS

The watchman who lifts up his soul to idols will have a more difficult time seeing in the spirit. An idol is anything that you put in God's place. For example, watching TV when He's telling you to watch in the spirit would be idolatrous. Money can be an idol. Family can be an idol. Anything that you let distract you from the assignment God has on your life can be an idol.

Paul told us to put to death any idolatry we find in our hearts (see Col. 3:5). John warned us to keep ourselves from idols (see 1 John 5:21). David warned that the sorrows of people who run after other gods will multiply (Ps. 16:4). Paul admonished us to flee from idolatry (see 1 Cor. 10:14). Idolatry is a work of the flesh (see Gal. 5:19-21). If you want to see in the spirit, you need to avoid works of the flesh, including idolatry.

Idolatry will blind you. Psalm 115:4-8 makes it clear:

> *Their idols are silver and gold, the work of men's hands. They have mouths, but they do not speak; eyes they have, but they do not see; they have ears, but they do not hear; noses they have, but they do not smell; they have hands, but they do not handle; feet they have, but they do not walk; nor do they mutter through their throat. Those who make them are like them; so is everyone who trusts in them.*

The Passion Translation puts Psalm 115:5-8 this way:

> *They idolize what they own and what they make with their hands, but their things can't talk to them or answer their prayers. Their possessions will never satisfy. Their futile faith in dead idols and dead works can never bring life or meaning to their souls. Blind men can only create blind things. Those deaf to God can only make a deaf image. Dead men can only create dead idols. And everyone who trusts in these powerless, dead things will be just like what they worship—powerless and dead.*

Catch that. *So is everyone who trusts in them.* If you serve idols, it blinds your eyes and more. Now consider this: Even your watchman's ministry can become an idol to you. One has to remember what Paul told the church at Colossae: Do everything you do as unto the Lord (see Col. 3:23). That even means watching. Although we should always be watchful, we shouldn't make an idol out of our ministry. We are not our ministry. We are sons and daughters of God. Too many have made an idol out of ministry and seen their families fall apart.

ARE YOU SWEARING DECEITFULLY?

The psalmist gives a last qualification for ascending—not swearing deceitfully. What does this mean, you might wonder? God is looking for a people, "whose hearts are true and sealed by the truth, those who never deceive, whose words are sure" (Ps. 24:4 TPT). *The Message* puts it this way: "Men who won't cheat, women who won't seduce."

God takes deceit seriously. As a matter of fact, "He who works deceit shall not dwell within my house; he who tells lies shall not continue in my presence" (Ps. 101:7). That should put the fear of the Lord into a watchman and cause him to cry out, "Deliver my soul, O Lord, from lying lips and from a deceitful tongue" (Ps. 120:2). If you want to ascend, you need to put away all deceit (see 1 Pet. 2:1).

BE SPIRITUALLY AWARE

Cultivating a watchman's eye means disciplining yourself to be spiritually aware. You might also call this spiritually awake. Jesus warned us to stay awake at all times (see Luke 21:36). That doesn't mean we can't sleep at night; it speaks of being spiritually aware of what is going on in the unseen realm. Jesus charged all believers with staying awake at all times. How much more so the watchman.

Paul wrote, "Accordingly then, let us not sleep, as the rest do, but let us keep wide awake (alert, watchful, cautious, and on our guard) and let us be sober (calm, collected, and circumspect)" (1 Thess. 5:6 AMPC). Paul also told the church at Ephesus to be "watchful to this end with all perseverance and supplication for all the saints" (Eph. 6:18), and Peter told us to "be self-controlled and sober-minded for the sake of your prayers" (1 Pet. 4:7 ESV).

In my book *Seer Activations* I offer over 100 activations to help you train your spiritual eyes. One of the activations is called "See Spiritual Awareness." This is part and parcel to developing a watchman's eye. Here is one of the entries that will help you:

According to *The Seer's Dictionary*, spiritual awareness is being intentionally aware of your spiritual surroundings, including discerning atmospheres, climates, spiritual warfare, and disturbances in the spirit; a state of being spiritual alert that comes from walking in the light of God (see Col. 1:3)

Jesus was aware of the reasonings of men's hearts. After He fed the masses with a few loaves and fishes, Jesus told His disciples to beware of the leaven of the Pharisees and the leaven of Herod. Mark 8:16-18 records:

> *And they reasoned among themselves, saying, "It is because we have no bread." But Jesus, being aware of it, said to them, "Why do you reason because you have no bread? Do you not yet perceive nor understand? Is your heart still hardened? Having eyes, do you not see? And having ears, do you not hear? And do you not remember?"*

Over and over again in Scripture, we see Jesus walked in spiritual awareness. You can practice this. Pray this prayer

> Father, in the name of Jesus, help me to be spiritually aware. Give me the grace to enter into a seer dimension in which I am aware of spiritual atmospheres, demonic agendas, the thoughts and intentions of people's hearts in situations. Teach me by Your Spirit to be spiritually aware as Jesus was when He walked in the earth.

Chapter 6

ENGAGING WITH ANGEL AND DEMON WATCHERS

W ATCHMEN watch and watchmen pray, but watchmen must also war. Spiritual warfare skills are an absolute necessity in the watchman's repertoire—a key issue in the making of a watchman. While the watchman never stops watching, the watchman's operations can suddenly shift according to what is happening in the spirit realm. The watchman, for example, may start out watching the war in the heavenlies from his station, discerning the spirits at work to oppose God's will, and swiftly find himself engaged in the battle against demon powers.

Watchmen, then, must become well-versed with spiritual warfare tactics and strategies that force him out of the scene. And beyond spiritual warfare 101, the watchman needs an understanding of the spirit beings they are watching for and warring against. Those spirit beings include various demonic personalities and principalities. Indeed, watchmen will encounter demonic resistance to watching and praying and must learn how to battle through to see, hear, and make intercession. Watchmen need to learn how to work with angels for ultimate success.

Engaging with angels and demons starts with the understanding that the watchman is in a war. Ephesians 6:12 tells us more about the warfare watchmen face:

> *For we are not wrestling with flesh and blood [contending only with physical opponents], but against the despotisms, against the powers, against [the master spirits who are] the world rulers of this present darkness, against the spirit forces of wickedness in the heavenly (supernatural) sphere* (AMPC).

THE WRESTLING WATCHMAN

Paul the apostle describes our combat with the devil as a wrestling match. Watchmen must become professionals in spiritual wrestling. Amateur wrestlers will struggle. The Greek word for *wrestling* in Ephesians 6:12 is *pallo*. *The New Testament KJV Greek Lexicon* defines it as, "a contest between two in which each endeavors to throw the other, and which is decided when the victor is able to hold his opponent down with his hand upon his neck; the term is transferred to the Christian's struggle with the power of evil."

Wrestling implies a close struggle. Naturally speaking, a wrestling match is a competition between two wrestlers. You can win by pinning your opponent to the mat, win by default if the opponent doesn't show up, win by injury, or win by disqualification. The enemy wants to pin you to the mat with oppression, fool you into not picking up your weapons, or tempt you into sin so he can disqualify you. Most of the wrestling you do with the enemy is in your mind.

Demons try to choke you—or put you in a stranglehold. In the wrestling world, a stranglehold is an illegal hold that chokes the opponent. *Merriam-Webster* calls it a "force or influence that chokes or suppresses freedom of movement or expression." If the wrestler doesn't break free from the stranglehold, the lack of blood or air can cause him to black out. Translating this to our spiritual realities, the enemy wants to choke the Word of God out of your mouth so you can't wield your sword of the Spirit or pray. The enemy wants to choke out the revelation of who you are in Christ and your authority over him.

We don't have the space in this book to go in-depth on spiritual warfare. I developed the School of Spiritual Warfare at SchooloftheSpirit.tv to teach 18 courses on this topic, and I have written many books. The key here is to bring awareness that the watchman has an enemy, an opponent to his mission. Paul tells us plainly in Second Corinthians 2:11 not to be ignorant of the devil's devices. The word *devices* in Second Corinthians 2:11 comes from the Greek word *noema*, according to the lexicon. It means a material perception, "a mental perception, thought; an evil purpose; that which thinks, the mind, thoughts or purposes."

The Greek word for *ignorant* in that verse is *agnoeo*, which in this context means "to be ignorant, not to know; not to understand, unknown," according to *The KJV New Testament Greek Lexicon*. We must be a student of God and His Word, but God warns about the enemy's nature, character, and ploys—and gives us clear examples of his machinations against the saints—throughout Scripture. Clearly, God does wants us to understand the enemy's devices. Some translations say "sly ways," "schemes," "designs," "intentions," and "thoughts."

God has given you weapons to push back the darkness. Paul said, "For the weapons of our warfare are not physical [weapons of flesh and blood], but they are mighty before God for the overthrow and destruction of strongholds" (2 Cor. 10:4 AMPC). The Passion Translation puts it this way:

For although we live in the natural realm, we don't wage a military campaign employing human weapons, using manipulation to achieve our aims. Instead, our spiritual weapons are energized with divine power to effectively dismantle the defenses behind which people hide.

WRESTLING DEMONIC WATCHERS

Beyond principalities, powers, rulers of the darkness and spiritual wickedness in high places that watchmen may have to wrestle in spiritual warfare, there are also demonic watchers that will work to spy out the watchman's plans. Maybe you've never heard of demonic watchers. Have you heard of watcher angels? The Bible speaks of watcher angels three times, all in the Book of Daniel.

Daniel 4:13 reads: "I saw in the visions of my head while on my bed, and there was a watcher, a holy one, coming down from heaven." Daniel 4:17 tells us:

This decision is by the decree of the watchers, and the sentence by the word of the holy ones, in order that the living may know that the Most High rules in the kingdom of men, gives it to whomever He will, and sets over it the lowest of men.

And Daniel 4:23 reveals:

And inasmuch as the king saw a watcher, a holy one, coming down from heaven and saying, "Chop down the tree

*and destroy it, but leave its stump and roots in the earth,
bound with a band of iron and bronze in the tender grass
of the field; let it be wet with the dew of heaven, and let
him graze with the beasts of the field, till seven times pass
over him."*

The Hebrew word for *watcher* in these verses is *iyr* (eer). According to *The KJV Old Testament Hebrew Lexicon*, it means, "waking, watchful, wakeful one, watcher, angel." The *International Standard Bible Encyclopedia* describes watcher angels as servants of God who "possess a certain joint authority to speak the decrees of God, and apparently form a heavenly council who listen to God's word and then act as divine messengers to bring these commands and revelations to human beings."

If there are watcher angels, don't you think there are watcher demons? The enemy counterfeits and perverts what God has established because he wants to be like God. God never created anything evil, but living creatures have a free will. We see the operation of a watcher demon assigned to Paul's ministry in Acts 16:16-19:

*Now it happened, as we went to prayer, that a certain
slave girl possessed with a spirit of divination met us, who
brought her masters much profit by fortune-telling. This
girl followed Paul and us, and cried out, saying, "These
men are the servants of the Most High God, who proclaim to us the way of salvation." And this she did for
many days.
But Paul, greatly annoyed, turned and said to the spirit,
"I command you in the name of Jesus Christ to come out of
her." And he came out that very hour. But when her masters saw that their hope of profit was gone, they seized Paul*

and Silas and dragged them into the marketplace to the authorities.

Yes, this was a spirit of divination. But it was also a watcher demon. Watcher demons can work through people, objects, animals, dogs, cats, birds, flies, and bees are common agents of these evil watchers. People influenced by a monitoring spirit will seek out information. They will ask more questions than are normal. They will insert themselves into your private affairs. If you share information with someone influenced by a monitoring spirit, you'll notice your plans are thwarted.

Watcher demons gather evidence against you to take to the courts of heaven and hold back your blessing. Watcher demons look for your weaknesses. Watcher demons report your words that are not in line with God's Word so the enemy can snare you with the words of your mouth (see Prov. 6:2). Watcher demons specifically empower the work of harassing spirits, hindering spirits, delay spirits, and sabotaging spirits. They feed these spirits information. Watcher demons can influence your thoughts through vain imaginations. Watcher demons are patient.

How do you deal with watcher demons? This could be a book in and of itself, but the bottom line is you bind them and blind them—release double fire against them. Decree Scriptures promising angelic protection. Watcher demons are entities watchmen have to guard against. I suggest saying a preemptive prayer before you set yourself on your guard post. You can pray this: "Father, in the name of Jesus, I bind and blind all monitoring spirits. I roast them with fire. Lord, release watcher angels to combat the watcher demons in my midst and eradicate them from my presence once and for all."

THE WATCHMAN-ANGEL PARTNERSHIP

Here's what we need to understand as watchman intercessors: Every prayer you pray is met with resistance. Sometimes you feel like your prayers are hitting a hard heaven because of the spiritual climate in a city. Sometimes you feel your prayers' answers are being held back. As I mentioned earlier, principalities and powers are going to resist your intercessory prayer answers because they do not want God to get the glory. God gets glory when your Spirit-inspired prayers are answered because His will is done on earth as it is in heaven.

But I have good news. Only one third of the angels are on satan's side. Two-thirds of the heavenly host did not follow lucifer in his insurrection and they are working for God and His people—and I'm not so sure God didn't create more to replace the ones He kicked out of heaven. Watchmen must come to understand the ministry of angels and how to work with angels to see God's will come to pass.

Whether or not you've ever seen an angel, you can understand their operations in the spirit realm. Hebrews 1:13-14 offers us some insight into their overall assignment in the earth in this age: "But to which of the angels has He ever said: 'Sit at My right hand, till I make Your enemies Your footstool'? Are they not all ministering spirits sent forth to minister for those who will inherit salvation?"

Angels are spirit beings. God sends them to minister to His people. In fact, twice in Scripture we see angels sent to strengthen Jesus—in the wilderness and in the Garden of Gethsemane. If Jesus received the ministry of angels, shouldn't we? Consider this: Demons minister against the heirs of salvation. Angels work for you. If I could pull back the curtain on the spirit realms, you would see an epic war going on. Watchmen need to learn how to work with angels.

BENEFITS OF A WATCHMAN-ANGEL PARTNERSHIP

Beyond watcher angels sharing messages with the watchmen, I've realized many benefits of working with angels. There are five key benefits in which we need to be confident: 1) angels don't sleep; 2) angels have supernatural strength; 3) angels are smart; 4) angels obey God; 5) angels travel at the speed of light. Let's explore each benefit.

Angels don't need to rest. Revelation 4:8 reveals: "The four living creatures had six wings each, and they were covered with eyes all around. All day and night, without ceasing, they were saying: "'Holy, holy, holy, Lord God Almighty,'" who was, and is, and is to come'" (MEV). Angels minister day and night without ceasing. Like God, they never sleep or slumber. We can't war and sleep at the same time, but angels can fight for us while we sleep. We get weary in the warfare. Angels don't get weary. Ever.

Angels have supernatural strength. Second Thessalonians 1:7 says angels are mighty and Revelation 18:1 tells us they have great power. Psalm 103:20 says they excel in strength. Demons have supernatural strength, and our human strength is no match for them. We can't go toe to toe with demons in our own strength, but warring angels can battle demons face to face.

Angels have an intellect and are wise. Second Samuel 14:20 speaks of the "wisdom of angels." Angels have the capability to think. Angels are not mindless spirits. Angels aren't heavenly robots that wait on every instruction from God to move in a battle. They aren't computer programmed. They have wisdom in warfare and they can strategize in the battle. Warring angels are experienced.

Angels are always obedient to God's Word. "Bless the Lord, you His angels, who are mighty, and do His commands, and obey the voice of His word" (Ps. 103:20 MEV). Angels will never leave you in the lurch. They will never betray God, and God will never betray you; therefore, angels will never leave you hanging.

Angels travel with lightning speed. Revelation 8 and 9 show angels moving rapidly through heaven. Angels are beings of light that move at light speed, which is 186,000 miles per second. Actually, it's been said angels travel at the speed of thought. These ministering spirits can be there to help you in the battle as fast as you can think about it.

Angels don't pray for us. Jesus Himself, a far greater one, is praying for us. But angels can fight the demons to bring us the prayer answers. Many of us believe all this, but we're not mindful of the angels while we're making intercession. Or we use rote prayers, like, "God, send Your angels." But we are not truly working with angels as a partnership, empowering them as agents on earth to do God's will.

WATCHMAN INTERCESSION RELEASES A WAR IN THE HEAVENS

Watchman intercession releases a war in the heavens. When we pray according to God's will, He hears and answers our prayers, according to First John 5:14. But we know the devil sometimes hears us pray and positions himself to interfere with the answer delivery. We also know the enemy sees things in the spirit we don't see. Demonic powers can clearly see the angels that are delivering your prayer answers or working behind the scenes to execute God's will even when you can't.

You're familiar with Daniel's intercession for Israel and what happened next. An angel came to visit him:

Then he said to me, "Do not fear, Daniel, for from the first day that you set your heart to understand, and to humble yourself before your God, your words were heard; and I have come because of your words. But the prince of the kingdom of Persia withstood me twenty-one days; and behold, Michael, one of the chief princes, came to help me, for I had been left alone there with the kings of Persia. Now I have come to make you understand what will happen to your people in the latter days, for the vision refers to many days yet to come" (Daniel 10:12-14).

Skipping down to Daniel 10:20-21, we see Daniel's conversation with the angel continue.

Then he said, "Do you know why I have come to you? And now I must return to fight with the prince of Persia; and when I have gone forth, indeed the prince of Greece will come. But I will tell you what is noted in the Scripture of Truth. (No one upholds me against these, except Michael your prince)."

We know this battle was 21 days. We also know some battles are longer than 21 days. This is why the watchman must stay in the wrestling match, tagging out with other intercessors as necessary. This is why, also, watchmen need to band together with intercessors. One can put a thousand to flight, and two can put ten thousand to flight (see Josh. 23:10).

Remember, the angel said he came for Daniel's words. Our words attract demons and angels. Some watchmen intercessors sound mighty in prayer but disbelief hits them when circumstances don't work out and they cancel out their prayers with words of frustration of fear. Again, our words attract demons and angels. Let that sink in.

YOU ARE THE VOICE OF GOD'S WORD

Bless the Lord, you His angels, who excel in strength, who do His word, heeding the voice of His word (Psalm 103:20).

You are the voice of God's Word in the earth, just like you are His body, His hands, His feet, etc. God can command dispatch angels in heaven to do His bidding in response to your prayers. He can answer a prayer however He chooses, but the angels also come for your words. The angels come to the voice of God's Word in your mouth.

The Passion Translation of Psalm 103:20 reads, "So bless the Lord, all his messengers of power, for you are his mighty heroes who listen intently to the voice of his word to do it." God's Word does not return to Him void, but it accomplishes what He sends it to do (see Isa. 55:11). God's Word will also accomplish what you send it to do, many times with the help of angels.

When you pray, speak, or decree the word in faith, angels' ears perk up and they set out to battle in the heavens against demonic interference. Remember how the intercessors worked with angels to help Peter get free? I doubt the intercessors understood they were working with angels, but that's what was happening. How much more confident and powerful can we be in prayer when we get the revelation that we're literally working with angels. Consider the impact of Peter's intercessors in Acts 12:1-11:

Now about that time Herod the king stretched out his hand to harass some from the church. Then he killed James the brother of John with the sword. And because he saw that it pleased the Jews, he proceeded further to seize Peter also. Now it was during the Days of Unleavened Bread. So when he had arrested him, he put him in prison, and delivered him to four squads of soldiers to keep him, intending to bring him before the people after Passover.

Peter was therefore kept in prison, but constant prayer was offered to God for him by the church. And when Herod was about to bring him out, that night Peter was sleeping, bound with two chains between two soldiers; and the guards before the door were keeping the prison. Now behold, an angel of the Lord stood by him, and a light shone in the prison; and he struck Peter on the side and raised him up, saying, "Arise quickly!" And his chains fell off his hands. Then the angel said to him, "Gird yourself and tie on your sandals"; and so he did. And he said to him, "Put on your garment and follow me." So he went out and followed him, and did not know that what was done by the angel was real, but thought he was seeing a vision. When they were past the first and the second guard posts, they came to the iron gate that leads to the city, which opened to them of its own accord; and they went out and went down one street, and immediately the angel departed from him.

And when Peter had come to himself, he said, "Now I know for certain that the Lord has sent His angel, and has delivered me from the hand of Herod and from all the expectation of the Jewish people."

You can also ask God to send angels to help you fight. Remember, watchman, you have angels assigned to you. Not all of them are warring angels, but some of us have warring angels on assignment for us depending on our call. Jesus had warring angels at His disposal. Matthew 26:51-53 reads:

> *And suddenly, one of those who were with Jesus stretched out his hand and drew his sword, struck the servant of the high priest, and cut off his ear. But Jesus said to him, "Put your sword in its place, for all who take the sword will perish by the sword. Or do you think that I cannot now pray to My Father, and He will provide Me with more than twelve legions of angels?"*

If God would do it for Jesus, He'll do it for you. First John 4:17 tells us as Jesus is, we are in this world. We have His delegated authority. We don't command angels or pray to them, but we can decree God's Word into a situation and angels will respond.

ACTIVATING ANGELS OF WAR

Also called warring angels, God sends angels on an assignment to fight for His people in times of war. In the Old Testament, we see examples of this in the physical realm. In the New Testament—in the Book of Revelation—we see a war in the heavens. Listen in to this startling account in Second Kings 19:34-35:

> *"For I will protect this city to save it, for My own sake and for the sake of David My servant." On that night the angel*

of the Lord went out and struck one hundred and eighty-five thousand in the camp of the Assyrians. When others woke up early in the morning, these were all dead bodies (MEV).

As mighty as David was in battle—after all, he defeated Goliath with a sling and a stone when the rest of the children of Israel were shaking in their boots and sang songs about how he slew tens of thousands (see 1 Sam. 18:7)—he still called on angels of war in times of distress. David prayed to the Lord to send angels on assignment to fight for him in war in Psalm 35. You'll notice how David depends on the Lord, but calls for the angels.

> *Plead my cause, O Lord, with my adversaries; fight those who fight me. Take hold of the large shield and small shield, and rise up for my help. Draw the spear and javelin against those who pursue me. Say to my soul, "I am Your salvation." May those who seek my life be ashamed and humiliated; may those who plan my injury be turned back and put to shame. May they be as chaff before the wind, and may the angel of the Lord cast them down. May their way be dark and slippery, and may the angel of the Lord pursue them. For without cause they have hidden their net for me in a pit, which they have dug without cause for my soul* (Psalm 35:1-7 MEV).

In the Book of Revelation, we read about an epic war between good and evil—a battle between the archangel Michael and his angels and a cohort of demons. The dramatic account is recorded in Revelation 12:6-8, demonstrating the warring nature of some angels on assignment:

The woman fled into the wilderness where she has a place prepared by God, that they may nourish her there for one thousand two hundred and sixty days. Then war broke out in heaven. Michael and his angels fought against the dragon, and the dragon and his angels fought, but they did not prevail, nor was there a place for them in heaven any longer.

ASK GOD TO OPEN YOUR EYES

When you start praying, the battle is on. If God pulled back the curtain on the spirit realm, you would see how your prayers fuel the battle. As a watchman, maybe you'll see it. Elisha's servant did.

In Elisha's day, the king of Syria was warring against Israel. The prophet Elisha gave the Israelites a marked advantage—he was able to hear the words Syria's king spoke in his bedroom and relayed them to the king of Israel (see 2 Kings 6:12). The Syrian king wanted Elisha stopped and sent out horses and chariots and a great army to fetch him. When he saw the Syrian army surrounded the city, Elisha's servant got scared.

And his servant said to him, "Alas, my master! What shall we do?" So he answered, "Do not fear, for those who are with us are more than those who are with them." And Elisha prayed, and said, "Lord, I pray, open his eyes that he may see." Then the Lord opened the eyes of the young man, and he saw. And behold, the mountain was full of horses and chariots of fire all around Elisha (2 Kings 6:15-17).

What confidence Elisha's servant must have gained—not just in that moment but throughout his walk with the Lord. And that brings me to Paul's prayer for the church at Ephesus, which is something I would suggest praying over yourself daily. In this prayer, Paul asks the Lord to open the believers' eyes for a specific purpose—a purpose that is sure to spark faith in soul and spirit:

> *Therefore I also, after I heard of your faith in the Lord Jesus and your love for all the saints, do not cease to give thanks for you, making mention of you in my prayers: that the God of our Lord Jesus Christ, the Father of glory, may give to you the spirit of wisdom and revelation in the knowledge of Him, the eyes of your understanding being enlightened; that you may know what is the hope of His calling, what are the riches of the glory of His inheritance in the saints, and what is the exceeding greatness of His power toward us who believe, according to the working of His mighty power* (Ephesians 1:15-19).

Chapter 7

WATCHING FOR THE KING OF GLORY

Y OU might get the idea that the watchman's ministry is all about warnings of sin, sounding alarms when danger is approaching, or discerning enemy attacks. Although that is the major thrust of the watchman's ministry, there's a lesser-discussed function that's just as important—watching for the King of Glory and His holy angels. The making of a modern-day watchman must have an emphasis on watching for the Lord.

Jesus rebuked the Pharisees for missing the day of their visitation (see Luke 19:44). God wants us to be aware of His presence so we can cooperate with the move of the Holy Spirit. He wants us to discern angelic activity so we can work with angels. If we're stuck on watching demons, we could miss the King of Glory. A balanced watchman sees the danger, but lifts up his eyes to see the glory of the Lord approaching to prepare a people for visitation. Psalm 24:7-10 tells us:

> *Lift up your heads, O you gates! And be lifted up, you ever-lasting doors! And the King of glory shall come in. Who is*

this King of glory? The Lord strong and mighty, the Lord mighty in battle. Lift up your heads, O you gates! Lift up, you everlasting doors! And the King of glory shall come in. Who is this King of glory? The Lord of hosts, He is the King of glory. Selah.

The watchman should be as proficient at seeing the approaching King of Glory as he is seeing the sin of mankind or the enemy prowling around like a roaring lion seeking someone to devour. But God's glory can manifest in many different ways. We have to understand the glory of God to rightly recognize it. Some years ago, at a time when we were usually seeing glory manifestations in our ministry, I prophesied about the glory of God.

> My glory is not to be taken lightly. My glory is not to be mocked. My glory is to be entered into with reverence, with holy fear and trembling, with awe. For I am indeed pouring out My glory more and more as the darkness begins to rise in the earth. I am determined that My people not only taste and see My glory, but walk in My glory to demonstrate to a lost world that I am a living God and a loving God.
>
> I am looking for carriers of My glory who will steward My presence and release My gifts without seeking their own glory. I am looking for those who will host My presence with Kingdom understanding and look beyond a single meeting to the transformative power of My Spirit in the earth. I am calling on you now to press into My glory, not for your sake but for the sake of the nations. My glory will indeed cover the earth like the waters cover the sea.

EZEKIEL WATCHED FOR GOD'S GLORY

When we think of Ezekiel, we're quick to point to the "blood on your hands" verses, but the watchman prophet was as much a glory watcher as a sin watcher. If you have the ability to see the sin and the demons, you have the ability to see the King of Glory and His angels. As a matter of fact, before Ezekiel was anointed as the "blood on your hands" watchman, he saw visions of God.

In Ezekiel 1, the vision starts with a whirlwind coming out of the north. He saw four living creatures, each with the likeness of man, each with four faces and four wings. What a sight! He goes into great detail about the four living creatures and what they did before going on to describe the vision of the wheel within a wheel, with rims full of eyes. It's a dramatic vision that should inspire watchmen and seers. Finally, in Ezekiel 1:26-28:

> *And above the firmament that was over their heads was the likeness of a throne in appearance like a sapphire stone, and seated above the likeness of a throne was a likeness with the appearance of a Man.*
>
> *From what had the appearance of His waist upward, I saw a lustre as it were glowing metal with the appearance of fire enclosed round about within it; and from the appearance of His waist downward, I saw as it were the appearance of fire, and there was brightness [of a halo] round about Him.*
>
> *Like the appearance of the bow that is in the cloud on the day of rain, so was the appearance of the brightness round about. This was the appearance of the likeness of the glory*

of the Lord. And when I saw it, I fell upon my face and I heard a voice of One speaking (AMPC).

Ezekiel saw the glory of God. I believe God gave him this experience before calling him to deal with the sin in the land so that he would have a proper perspective. While watchmen deal with a lot of demons, we have to learn how to keep God at the center of our focus. God is omnipresent. He is everywhere all the time. In Psalm 139:7-12, David wrote:

> *Where can I go from Your Spirit? Or where can I flee from Your presence? If I ascend into heaven, You are there; if I make my bed in hell, behold, You are there. If I take the wings of the morning, and dwell in the uttermost parts of the sea, even there Your hand shall lead me, and Your right hand shall hold me. If I say, "Surely the darkness shall fall on me," even the night shall be light about me; indeed, the darkness shall not hide from You, but the night shines as the day; the darkness and the light are both alike to You.*

THE KNOWLEDGE OF THE GLORY

After years of my ministry being marked by spiritual warfare, I became a student of the glory of God. The Bible uses various words for glory over 350 times. It's one of the foundational themes in Scripture. The easiest definition of glory is God's manifest presence. In that presence, He demonstrates His goodness and His power through signs, wonders, and miracles. It's important to discern the glory of God or we will miss our visitation. Ruth Ward Heflin wrote:

The glory of God is bringing revival, and if we want more revival we must make room for the glory. This is the greatest need of the hour. ...Our failure to make room for the glory in our services is the most common reason that the glory is not seen and experienced in church after church across America and around the world. I believe that most of the necessary elements are in place, but we simply don't give God a chance. We don't make room for Him to work. We don't make room for the glory. ...When you discover things that seem to contribute to the glory, do those things more; and when you find things that seem to diminish the glory, stop doing them. It's as simple as that.[1]

What I've discovered through study and practical experience is that the glory of God manifests in many different ways. You may discern it in your spirit or see in the spirit the glory of God in more than one realization.

SET A FIRE DOWN IN MY SOUL

When I was in Singapore in 2017, the Lord assigned fire angels to me. We know the Angel of the Lord appeared to Moses in a flame of fire in a bush (see Exod. 3:2). And Psalm 104:4 calls angels spirits who are "a flame of fire." In Revelation 14:18, the Bible speaks of an angel who has power of fire. Ever since God assigned angels of fire, I've seen fire manifestations of glory in my ministry. I can sense those angels of fire.

The Bible makes a direct connection between fire and glory again and again. We first see this in Exodus 24:17: "The sight of the glory of the Lord was like a consuming fire on the top of the mountain in the eyes of the children of Israel." And again in Deuteronomy 5:24:

And you said: "Surely the Lord our God has shown us His glory and His greatness, and we have heard His voice from the midst of the fire. We have seen this day that God speaks with man; yet he still lives."

Fire represents the purifying power of God—holiness. Visions of God in His glory across the pages of the Bible—both Old and New Testaments—showcase fire. Zechariah 2:5 reveals, "'For I,' says the Lord, 'will be a wall of fire all around her, and I will be the glory in her midst.'" And Isaiah 10:16 reads: "Therefore the Lord, the Lord of hosts, will send leanness among his fat ones; and under his glory He will kindle a burning like the burning of a fire." After the Solomon dedicated the temple:

Fire came down from the heavens and consumed the burnt offering and sacrifices, and the glory of the Lord filled the temple. And the priests were not able to enter into the house of the Lord, for the glory of the Lord filled the Lord's house. And all the sons of Israel saw when the fire came down and the glory of the Lord came on the temple, and they bowed their faces low to the ground on the pavement, and they worshipped confessing, "The Lord is good, and His mercy endures forever" (2 Chronicles 7:1-3 MEV).

VISIBLE GLORY CLOUDS

I have seen glory clouds on many occasions. The first time was the most striking because, well, it was the first time. I was ministering in Nicaragua. Actually, I was running the camera in the meeting when I saw what looked like a mist or haze between me and the preacher. It was like a wall of mist that seemed thick, yet translucent at the same time. I tried to photograph it but it did not show up on film. The preacher later told me it was the glory of God.

We see what we call the "glory cloud" as one of the first visual manifestations of God's glory in the Bible. Exodus 13:21 recounts, "The Lord went before them by day in a pillar of cloud to lead them along the way, and by night in a pillar of fire, to give them light, so that they might travel by day and by night" (MEV). And in Exodus 16:10:

Now it came to pass, as Aaron spoke to the whole congregation of the children of Israel, that they looked toward the wilderness, and behold, the glory of the Lord appeared in the cloud.

The Bible doesn't stop there. Exodus 24:16 shares, "Now the glory of the Lord rested on Mount Sinai, and the cloud covered it six days. And on the seventh day He called to Moses out of the midst of the cloud." And Exodus 40:34-35 reads:

Then the cloud covered the tabernacle of meeting, and the glory of the Lord filled the tabernacle. And Moses was not able to enter the tabernacle of meeting, because the cloud rested above it, and the glory of the Lord filled the tabernacle.

You might think, "Well, that was just an Exodus thing. It's part of the signs and wonders God showed to His people through the deliverance from the Egyptians." No, we see glory clouds again in Numbers 16:42:

> *Now it happened, when the congregation had gathered against Moses and Aaron, that they turned toward the tabernacle of meeting; and suddenly the cloud covered it, and the glory of the Lord appeared.*

And in case you are saying, "Well, that was just a Moses thing," consider First Kings 8:10-11, "And it came to pass, when the priests came out of the holy place, that the cloud filled the house of the Lord, so that the priests could not continue ministering because of the cloud; for the glory of the Lord filled the house of the Lord." And Ezekiel 1:28, "Like the appearance of a rainbow in a cloud on a rainy day, so was the appearance of the brightness all around it. This was the appearance of the likeness of the glory of the Lord. So when I saw it, I fell on my face, and I heard a voice of One speaking."

It's true that some people claim glory clouds do not exist. However, glory clouds are real and you can see them with your natural eyes. That said, I have discovered that not everyone can see the glory clouds I see, which tells me there are times when I am seeing the clouds in the spirit before they manifest in the natural dimension.

THE SOUND OF GLORY

When I was in Virginia ministering, I saw lightnings in my spirit and heard thunder. That's when I learned that glory can manifest as a sound. Perhaps the most known example is on the Day of Pentecost at the birth of the church. Acts 2:1-4 recounts the historic day:

When the Day of Pentecost had fully come, they were all with one accord in one place. And suddenly there came a sound from heaven, as of a rushing mighty wind, and it filled the whole house where they were sitting. Then there appeared to them divided tongues, as of fire, and one sat upon each of them. And they were all filled with the Holy Spirit and began to speak with other tongues, as the Spirit gave them utterance.

Can you imagine hearing that sound? Many times in Scripture, the Spirit-inspired authors did not have adequate words to describe what they were seeing, hearing, or feeling. They did the best they could—and so do we. Ezekiel must have struggled to find words to describe what he experienced, but he wrote, "And behold, the glory of the God of Israel came from the way of the east. His voice was like the sound of many waters; and the earth shone with His glory" (Ezek. 43:2).

In Exodus, we see a dramatic scene with sound, visuals, and fire. Try to imagine this as you read it:

Then it came to pass on the third day, in the morning, that there were thunderings and lightnings, and a thick cloud on the mountain; and the sound of the trumpet was very loud, so that all the people who were in the camp trembled. And Moses brought the people out of the camp to meet with God, and they stood at the foot of the mountain. Now Mount Sinai was completely in smoke, because the Lord descended upon it in fire. Its smoke ascended like the smoke of a furnace, and the whole mountain quaked greatly. And when the blast of the trumpet sounded long and became louder and louder, Moses spoke, and God answered him by voice (Exodus 19:16-19).

WHEN GLORY FALLS LIKE RAIN

Have you ever seen it raining on the inside? At my first women's conference at Awakening House of Prayer, we saw it rain on the inside. It was the glory of God. The result—every woman with any kind of ailment was healed. We saw miracles in the glory. I believe the rain comes out of the glory cloud, whether you can see it or not.

Job 37:11 says God loads the thick clouds with moisture. And Zechariah 10:1 says, "Ask for rain from the Lord during the season of the latter spring rains. And the Lord will make the storm winds; and He will give them showers of rain; all will have vegetation in the field." You can expect many of things in the rain of God's glory. On a morning prayer call the Lord once announced a season of rain. Here's what the Lord said to me:

> I will shower from above and the rain clouds will rain down righteousness and blessing upon you. You have waited and you have wanted and you have even wandered around in a desert place, a land of cracked, dry ground. But I called you in that season to break up the fallow ground so that I could prepare it, so that I could prepare you for the rain showers that are coming, the blessings that would come down like a deluge.
>
> I will flood your heart with blessings, and I will flood your mind with revelations, and you will come to see and

know that what the enemy meant for harm I intended for good. In this next season, the season of the rain, you will make up for lost time. And where you were thirsty and where you were hungry for the blessing, you will hunger and thirst for righteousness only. For the blessing will chase you down and overtake you.

And you will not have to wonder and worry any more about where the blessing will come from. Whatever the blessing is, whatever it is you need, whatever it is you want, whatever desires I have put in your heart—you will begin to see some of these things come to pass even from decades past. The enemy has shut up the heavens over your life for a little too long, and I have heard your cries and I have come down to deliver you and to bring the rain.

BRIGHT WHITE LIGHT

One definition of glory is light, so it's not surprising that God would manifest His glory as bright white light. When my daughter was a small girl, I prayed in her room against evil spirits—to evict them. At the end of the prayer, a bright white light shone in the room. God was manifesting His glory as a sign that His light displaced the darkness.

We see the glory of the Lord connected with light in Ezekiel 10:1-5:

And I looked, and there in the firmament that was above the head of the cherubim, there appeared something like a sapphire stone, having the appearance of the likeness of a throne. Then He spoke to the man clothed with linen, and said, "Go in among the wheels, under the cherub, fill your hands with coals of fire from among the cherubim, and scatter them over the city." And he went in as I watched.

Now the cherubim were standing on the south side of the temple when the man went in, and the cloud filled the inner court. Then the glory of the Lord went up from the cherub, and paused over the threshold of the temple; and the house was filled with the cloud, and the court was full of the brightness of the Lord's glory. And the sound of the wings of the cherubim was heard even in the outer court, like the voice of Almighty God when He speaks.

One of the most remarkable manifestations of God's glory as light happened after I hiked up into the Smokey Mountains of North Carolina. It was an arduous climb and exhausting. The day after this hike I ventured out onto a rock that extended into the river to sit in silence. The water was rushing and every now and then some of the freezing waves would crash on to the rock. As I sat in silence, the Lord told me to dip in the river seven times and He would peel away issues that hindered me from receiving His love.

I thought, *No way, that water is freezing.* Honestly, I had only been saved about two years. I didn't even know the story of Naaman the leper and Elisha's instruction for the Syrian army commander to wash in the river seven times. I thought it sounded strange, but I knew it was the Lord and obeyed. I think I screamed seven times, once for each time I dipped my body into the icy water.

After all that screaming and the freezing baptism, I was out of breath. I had no towel, so I laid on the rock. Suddenly, light from heaven shone down on me. The light was full of warmth. I was not cold anymore. It was the bright white light of the Lord warming me. That experience, I will never forget. Before he was Paul the apostle, Saul the Pharisee had a glory encounter I'm sure he'll never forget. We read it in Acts 9:1-9:

> *Then Saul, still breathing threats and murder against the disciples of the Lord, went to the high priest and asked letters from him to the synagogues of Damascus, so that if he found any who were of the Way, whether men or women, he might bring them bound to Jerusalem. As he journeyed he came near Damascus, and suddenly a light shone around him from heaven. Then he fell to the ground, and heard a voice saying to him, "Saul, Saul, why are you persecuting Me?"*
>
> *And he said, "Who are You, Lord?" Then the Lord said, "I am Jesus, whom you are persecuting. It is hard for you to kick against the goads." So he, trembling and astonished, said, "Lord, what do You want me to do?"*
>
> *Then the Lord said to him, "Arise and go into the city, and you will be told what you must do." And the men who journeyed with him stood speechless, hearing a voice but seeing no one. Then Saul arose from the ground, and when his eyes were opened he saw no one. But they led him by the hand and brought him into Damascus. And he was three days without sight, and neither ate nor drank."*

DUST, WIND, AND OIL

There are many other manifestations of God's glory. Some are visible, and some are invisible.

For example, I believe the glory dust comes out of the glory clouds, whether you can see the cloud or not. We've had glory dust appear in our Bibles at Awakening House of Prayer. This is biblical. Isaiah 60:2 tells us, "For the darkness shall cover the earth and deep darkness the peoples; but the Lord shall rise upon you, and His glory shall be seen upon you" (MEV).

In the 1970s, Kathryn Kuhlmann invited a foreign couple to come up to the platform. She told them, "The Lord has something for you." As they started coming, a strong wind blew and made it difficult for them to keep walking forward. They had to lean forward so they wouldn't fall over. Their clothes were flapping in the wind. The wind was only blowing in the center aisle. Kathryn thought it was funny and told them, "Don't be afraid, dear ones, that's the wind of the Holy Spirit blowing on you."

I haven't aimed to exhaust the whole list. We've seen oil on hands, weeping, feelings of electric shock waves, falling out in the spirit. Yes, there are excesses and even fakes in the realm of glory. But we can't deny it. The watchmen must look for signs of the King of Glory coming so we can prepare to receive Him in all His glory.

NOTE

1. Ruth Ward Heflin, *Revival Glory* (Hagerstown, MD: McDougal Publishing Company, 1998), 239, 190.

Chapter 8

PRACTICAL WAYS
TO WATCH

MY watch starts at 4 a.m.—or technically about 4:20 after the caffeine wakes up my brain. I figure if Jesus rose up early in the morning to pray and saw what the Father was doing, it's a good strategy for me. We don't know what time Jesus got up, but we know it was still dark outside.

My advantage in this watch is that it's still, which is one of the keys to active watching. The psalmist said, "Early will I seek thee" (Ps. 63:1 KJV). Of course, there are many watches to which God can assign you. In some ways, I'd much prefer the night watch as I have a bent toward staying up late and getting up even later. But God graces us for the watch to which He calls us.

Beyond Habakkuk climbing into his watchtower to see what God would say, the Bible doesn't offer us much instruction on how to actually watch. But watching in the spirit has a practical side as well as a spiritual side. In some ways, you learn by doing. There's no particular formula for watching, but I have learned principles of practical watching over the years. Remember this—all watching starts and ends with prayer.

BUILD YOUR TOWER IN PRAYER

The concept of a war room was made popular by a Christian movie of the same name. I love the war room, but the war room is different from the watchtower. Every watchman needs his own personal, private watchtower. You can't build my watchtower, and I can't build yours. You can't stand in my watchtower, and I can't stand in yours.

Like prophets, watchmen are not always the most popular ministry gift on the block because they are bold enough to release a word of the Lord that warns the local church of potentially unpleasant circumstances coming down the proverbial pike. In order to properly carry this mantle, genuine watchmen must build towers of prayer.

Watchmen may not win any popularity contests in the local church— or the Body of Christ at large—but they will sacrifice to make intercession. Building a watchtower in the spirit allows you to see the assignments coming against the church. Then you take that revelation and use it as spiritual mortar to make up a hedge in prayer against the assignment.

Prayer is the foundation of a watchman's ministry, and really the foundation of every Christian's relationship with God. It's through a strong prayer life that you connect deeply with God. The more you pray, the more sensitive to the Lord you're going to be. You have a gift, but you have to operate out of relationship, not just a gift or anointing. So build your tower in prayer. What does that mean? How do you build a tower of prayer?

Specifically, start by praying for God to show you what He wants you to see. Remember, even as a watchman you can only see what He allows you to see. You can't force your way into the spirit dimensions with God's blessing. Jesus is the Door, and if you are going to see in the spirit or discern operations of demons, it's by His invitation, grace, or gifts. There are illegal watchman operations, which are akin to divination. You can read more about divination in my book *Discerning Prophetic Witchcraft*.

Also ask for discernment, understanding, and wisdom. You want to discern rightly, understand what to do with what you see, and possess the wisdom to share it in the right way, with the right people, at the right time. Finally, pray in the Spirit. That is, pray in tongues. Praying in tongues builds you up in your most holy faith (see Jude 20). Praying in the spirit helps you watch. You're sowing to the spirit and you will reap from the spirit (see Gal. 6:8). It's a prayer secret every watchman needs in his arsenal. You can read more about this in my book *Your End Time Prayer Secret*.

STAY FOCUSED

Did you know humans have 70,000 thoughts a day? It can be hard to stay focused, especially when you are not immediately seeing anything. There's a thrill in seeing and hearing, and it's not as exciting to wait until you learn how to wait with expectation. In my School of the Seers, I teach on seer focus, and this applies to the watchman as well.

In my mid-twenties, I enrolled in photography school. Previously trained as a journalist, I set out to add to my repertoire of skills by learning how to wield a camera as well as a pen. I figured covering a presidential race or a sporting event from a words-and-picture perspective would give me an edge in a competitive industry—and I loved the creative side of photography.

My photography training was old school. We worked in the dark room to process black and white film using three sets of chemicals—developer, stop, and fix. Although digital cameras and accurate auto-focus features existed, they were not yet mainstream.

Part of my education was to learn to focus manually and set the aperture for the appropriate depth of field. During my time in photography school, I learned one could have the perfect exposure and a head-turning, emotion-driving subject, but if the photo is out of focus it is useless. Even photos that were slightly out of focus would not appear in newspapers or magazines. The focus had to be sharp, crystal clear, so the readers could truly appreciate the image I was capturing through the lens on my camera.

If you don't stay focused, you may miss what God is showing you. Or you may only catch a glimpse. You may miss part of the picture. Partial information can lead to disinformation. The biggest enemy to focus is distraction. The enemy will work to distract you from watching with thoughts, imaginations, itching ears, weary eyes, ringing phones, noisy neighbors, or anything else that works. Find a quiet place to watch and work to eliminate anything that will break your focus.

WATCH THE NEWS

Many people remember me as the senior editor of *Charisma* magazine, but fewer know I was a secular journalist for 25 years before I entered full-time ministry. I worked for the *New York Times*, the Associated Press, major magazines, and other secular media outlets for decades. I am trained to pay attention to the news. In fact, to this day I review the news headlines every morning to see what God will say to me or how He may lead me to pray for what is going on in the world.

It's vital that watchmen know what is happening in society. I understand all too well that the secular media twists and even perverts the truth. That's why I read the headlines. I can see quickly by scanning Google News what media around the world are saying. I can see reports of earthquakes or major world events coming down the pike. I can see what's going on in my city. I can see the health trends, technology trends, and the like. Many times, that will spark a prayer assignment.

"All too often, Christians feel powerless and at the mercy of a very big world. Watching or reading of news events can feel like an exercise in futility and even worse, bring a sense of anxiety and worry into our lives. One way to deal with this is to shut yourself off from the world. Turn off the television news and unsubscribe to your daily newspaper. Doing so may provide temporary relief, but certainly does nothing to change the situation," says Dave Butts, founder of Harvest Prayer Ministries.

"There is a better way. It involves a commitment to change your world through prayer. It happens as you see God's commitment to prayer as a change agent. You begin to see yourself as a player on the world stage. Rather than passively watching and worrying, or ignoring and hiding, you begin to take significant action to bring God's power to bear on situations going on in the world. You pray!

"The Bible is filled with examples of God's people watching political and national events unfold around them, and then intervening through prayer to bring change. Sometimes a national leader, such as King Asa or King Jehoshaphat of Judah, prayed when faced with a crisis. In both cases, a military attack against the nation was overcome by the prayer of a godly leader."[1]

Consider this: Rees Howells prayed the news. When he got news of the Nazi's movements, it fueled his prayer. The key is to see the news from God's perspective so you can pray with His heart. Use His discernment to fuel your prayer. You can't pray over every headline every day. You are scanning and watching for a headline to stir your spirit. Stay informed. You can't have your head in the sand and stand in your watchtower at the same time.

Wendy Griffith and Craig von Buseck, co-authors of *Praying the News*, wrote:

> When people pray in sincerity and unity according to the will of God revealed in the Bible, things change; headlines change. The ancient words of the apostle James are just as true today as they were when he wrote them under the inspiration of the Holy Spirit in the first century AD: "The effective prayer of a righteous man can accomplish much." ...We have seen the truth of this scriptural admonition powerfully demonstrated in recent events that have affected every person living on planet Earth.[2]

CONSULT THE WORD

Watchmen should always carry their sword—the Word of God—into the tower. Savvy watchmen consult the Word often. It helps open your eyes, renew your mind, confirm what you are seeing, and instruct you on what to do with what you've discerned. The Word can bring comfort, confirmation, and consultation. Consult the Word as a watchman and you'll stay grounded no matter what you see.

PAY ATTENTION TO PROMPTINGS

We want to live and walk by the Spirit (see Gal. 5:25). That means more than being aware of what is going on around you but what is going on in you. We have to learn to discern the Holy Spirit's leanings and promptings. *Prompt* means to move to action or to incite. It's a spiritual inspiration or spurring on to good works. You may see many things, but the Holy Spirit will lead you to look at specific things. Pay attention to the promptings.

One way the Holy Spirit prompts you is through peace, but the absence of peace can also be a signal that the Spirit of God within you is grieved. Likewise, an inner feeling of grief or despair can tune you into the emotions of the Holy Spirit. A sense of being on high alert can be a Spirit prompting. Maybe you feel there's something not quite right—is that the Holy Spirit prompting you?

Ultimately, we have to discern how the Holy Spirit leads or prompts generally but then also how He leads or prompts us individually. When something in the natural stands out to you above all its surroundings, that could be the Holy Spirit prompting you to take a closer look and to listen. An impression or a random thought could be the Holy Spirit's prompting to move in a certain direction to see more clearly.

Learning to discern how the Holy Spirit prompts you to watch, look, see, pray, and say comes with experience. Always test the spirits to make sure it's Him (see 1 John 4:1). Demons and your own mind will also prompt you at times. Always, always, always respond to the prompting of the Holy Spirit to watch and pray. Don't quench the prompting of the Holy Spirit in your watchman ministry or you could miss a critical message.

BREAK DOWN COMMUNICATION SILOS

Watchmen, prayer warriors, and intercessors need to come together. We must break down the communication silos. It's difficult in a busy world to get everyone together in person to share notes and pray.

Thankfully, there are online forums, group phone calls, Zoom, and other ways to share prophetic intelligence. We do this as part of my Ignite network (ignitenow.org). We know in part, but when we come together to share and pray, we can tap into a corporate anointing that sets an atmosphere and opens the heavens so revelation pours out. (You can also join the Prophetic Intelligence Network at propheticintel.com.)

Corporate decrees send the enemy packing. You've heard about the concept of corporate prayer and corporate worship, but corporate decrees kick it up a notch. You can build a flight team through corporate decrees. What is a flight team? We find this concept in Leviticus 26:8, "Five of you shall chase a hundred, and a hundred of you shall put ten thousand to flight, and your enemies shall fall before you by the sword" (MEV).

We first see this concept in Deuteronomy 32:30: "How should one chase a thousand, and two put ten thousand to flight" (MEV), and later we see another witness to its power in Joshua 23:10: "One man from among you can make a thousand flee, for it is the Lord your God who wages war for you, as He told you" (MEV).

KEEP A JOURNAL

Remember when Habakkuk was standing at his watch? The Lord answered him and said:

Write the vision and make it plain on tablets, that he may run who reads it. For the vision is yet for an appointed time; but at the end it will speak, and it will not lie. Though it tarries, wait for it; because it will surely come, it will not tarry (Habakkuk 2:2-3).

God told Hosea to write down what he saw. You may forget it if you don't write it down, or at least forget significant details that could later inform prayer. If you don't write it down and you may leave an important element out of the warning. *The Message* puts Habakkuk 2:2 this way: "Write it out in big block letters so that it can be read on the run. This vision-message is a witness pointing to what's coming."

Even if no one listens to your warning, when events unfold according to the words you released it will justify you. Maybe they will listen next time. Hopefully, visions of evil will not come to pass because intercessors will pick up the warning and war against it even if others reject the warning. Keeping a journal is not a way to prove your accuracy later, but to be accurate in what you release now so intercessors will hear a clear word and respond with a loud cry. A journal also helps you track your own accuracy privately so you can gain confidence or ask the Lord how you missed it if you missed it.

WHEN YOUR EYES ARE EXHAUSTED

While sharing this message at a roundtable of prophets in Windsor, England, one young prophet asked me this: "How do prophets and watchmen deal with exhaustion, especially exhaustion that's rooted in disappointment—spiritual exhaustion?" This young man said, at times, he felt what he could best describe as exasperation.

Indeed, being a watchman can be exhausting and exasperating. How did I answer him? The best answer from the Bible is found in Isaiah 40:29-31:

> *He gives power to the faint and weary, and to him who has no might He increases strength [causing it to multiply and making it to abound]. Even youths shall faint and be weary, and [selected] young men shall feebly stumble and fall exhausted; but those who wait for the Lord [who expect, look for, and hope in Him] shall change and renew their strength and power; they shall lift their wings and mount up [close to God] as eagles [mount up to the sun]; they shall run and not be weary, they shall walk and not faint or become tired* (AMPC).

Sometimes, we just need to rest. Other times, exhaustion is a sign of spiritual attack. Witchcraft, a force of the enemy that watchmen encounter, can leave you exhausted. If the enemy can't attack you by day, he'll often attack you at night and weaken you from lack of sleep. Don't you know it's so much more difficult to work with one hand and battle with the other when you are physically exhausted?

If you've slept eight hours, had a tall cup of coffee, and you still feel like you've been run over by a truck, witchcraft could be attacking you. This is one of the ways witchcraft comes after me. I've learned not to give in by laying down for a nap that turns into four or five hours of witchcraft-induced sleep. If you are eating well, sleeping well, exercising well, and living well—and if you are generally healthy—you shouldn't feel like you're walking through quicksand. This could be a witchcraft attack.

LEARNING TO CARRY PRAYER BURDENS

If you don't know how to carry a prayer burden, it can also be exhausting. The enemy can cover you with oppression as a form of retaliation in the very act of intercession. Intercession, for all intents and purposes, is an act of war. You are often standing between the people and the promise as you work to push back darkness trying to overshadow God's glory. As intercessors, though, you have to learn to discern between enemy oppression, your emotions, and a true prayer burden.

I wrote this on my Facebook page many years ago:

Intercessors, as we move deeper and deeper into the things of God, it's increasingly vital to learn to divide soul from spirit. When the burden of the Lord comes upon you, you may feel the weight of oppression, hear the enemy's accusations, or experience various negative emotions seemingly out of the blue. That's not you! Learn to quickly discern the call to pray against a thing rather than coming up under it.

You may be asking, "What is a prayer burden? Didn't Jesus say He would take our burdens, not give us burdens?" A prayer burden is not like a care of the world that keeps your soul in turmoil. A prayer burden is a spiritual load. A burden is something you carry, but with a prayer burden you are not carrying it alone. The Holy Spirit helps you carry it. When you have no idea how to pray, the Holy Spirit helps you (see Rom. 8:26-27).

A prayer burden is a God-assigned duty or responsibility to make intercession. The prayer burden will not lift until the assignment is complete—until heaven has heard and answered the prayer. You may see no evidence in the natural that the prayer is answered, but it's a done deal in heaven. It's important to recognize a prayer burden, first and foremost, so you can pray. It's also important to recognize when a prayer burden lifts so you can move on to the next assignment. All told, we must learn how to carry prayer burdens.

In his classic book *The Necessity of Prayer*, E.M. Bounds wrote:

Without desire, there is no burden of soul, no sense of need, no ardency, no vision, no strength, no glow of faith. There is no mighty pressure, no hold on to God, with a deathless, despairing grasp— "I will not let Thee go, except Thou bless me." There is no utter self-abandonment, as there was with Moses, when, lost in the throes of a desperate, pertinacious, and all-consuming plea he cried: "Yet now, if Thou wilt forgive their sin; if not, blot me, I pray Thee, out of Thy book." Or, as there was with John Knox when he pleaded: "Give me Scotland, or I die!"[3]

DIVIDING BETWEEN SOUL AND SPIRIT

We all have rough days. Overwhelming days. It's important as a watchman that you learn to quickly divide between soul and spirit. In other words, are we feeling down and out, depressed, or on high alert because we're having a bad day or because we're picking up on a prayer burden that we can't express with mere words? Are we oppressed because we're oppressed? Or are we are feeling the oppression in the atmosphere so we can stand in the gap for a people group?

I'm reminded of a trip to London in March 2020. I went to London to plant Awakening House of Prayer campuses and establish a School of Prophets almost every month during 2019. Our monthly visits were tapering off and we were planning quarterly trips to fuel the works we started. It should have been a victory, but I felt some sort of sting. At first, I could not discern it.

As I was walking to a restaurant down the streets of South London, I began to feel as if I was losing something. I felt like when I left London, I might never return—that I may never walk the streets again. It was overwhelming to the point that I teared up through dinner. I explained to my friend how I was feeling and told her, quite honestly, I couldn't really put exact words to the feeling and I wasn't sure in that moment if it was my soul or my spirit. I talked it out, then I prayed it out. I also sought the Word.

See, God's Word is an anchor for our soul (see Heb. 6:19). The Word of God keeps us grounded when we feel instability or we aren't sure the source of an emotion. And Hebrews 4:12 tells us:

> *For the Word that God speaks is alive and full of power [making it active, operative, energizing, and effective]; it is sharper than any two-edged sword, penetrating to the dividing line of the breath of life (soul) and [the immortal] spirit, and of joints and marrow [of the deepest parts of our nature], exposing and sifting and analyzing and judging the very thoughts and purposes of the heart* (AMPC).

The Word itself divides between soul and spirit. So when you aren't sure if you are having an emotional response to something or it's the Holy Spirit's emotions manifesting as a prayer burden, the first thing to do is get in the Word of God. I didn't know fully what it was for a few days. But about ten days after we left London, Europe went on lockdown due to the coronavirus. It will be many months before we can go back again.

But more than that, it's the pain and death people there are experiencing that I was feeling. So I pray.

THE ENEMY'S DECEPTION

The enemy wants us to default to the soul. He wants to trick us into believing the prayer burden is a disturbance in our mind, will, and emotions. He wants us to sit and feel sorry for ourselves and agree with the subtle suggestions he's making to inspire our emotions. We have to resist the enemy when we are attacked with oppression. We should cast down vain imaginations. But if it's a prayer burden, you can't cast it down—and why would you want to?

If you resist a prayer burden, you are resisting God because it's God who is allowing you to feel His feelings—or sometimes the feelings of those to whom you are assigned to pray. He may give you a burden for the city, and you will feel the emotions of people there who are crying out to God for deliverance.

This happened when I was in Nicaragua in the early 2000s. I was getting ready to join the prayer meeting when I felt a heavy oppression. I had no idea what was going on. I asked the Lord, "What is the matter with me? I was happy a minute ago." The Holy Spirit told me it was despondency, and it wasn't my feeling—it was the emotion of the people in Nicaragua who were facing desperate times. When I went into corporate prayer in the atrium, the burden lifted.

Watchman, be faithful to obey the unction. You will not be a successful and effective watchman if you think it's all about you. Sometimes it's easy to discern because your mood suddenly swings, like mine did in Nicaragua. Sometimes, it's more subtle. You may never know exactly who or what you were praying for, though as a watchman it's usually connected to something He showed you. You grow in this through experience.

NOTES

1. Dave Butts, "Praying the News," Harvest Prayer Ministries, https://www.harvestprayer.com/resources/personal-2/praying-the-news.

2. Wendy Griffith and Craig von Buseck, *Praying the News* (Ventura, CA: Regal Books, 2011), 14

3. E.M. Bounds, *The Necessity of Prayer* (New Kensington, PA: Whitaker House, 1984), 16.

Chapter 9

SOUNDING THE ALARM AND BLOWING THE TRUMPET

I N April 2017, the Holy Spirit sparked an urgency in my spirit to sound an alarm for France. It would be the first of many alarms He would lead me to sound in an effort to gather intercessors to cover the revival history-rich nation. I could not see the entirety of the enemy's plan at the first stirring, but I heard the Lord say:

> The enemy has marked France for destruction because of its spiritual heritage. If My intercessors will rise up and build a spiritual wall around the nation—raise up impenetrable borders around the country through repentance and praise—I Myself will raise up a standard that will stem the tide of this onslaught.
>
> I Myself will rise up and cause France's enemies to be scattered. I Myself will empower the politicians and police with strategies to eradicate terrorists from the land and thwart future attacks. I Myself will do it.
>
> So begin to pray now with greater fervor because lives are at stake, economies are at stake, and your spiritual

> heritage is at stake. Begin to cooperate now with My grace and My agenda and My plan for your nation, and I myself will fight with you and for you.

Fast-forward about two years, and I received yet another warning in 2019. When I stepped into Paris, I heard the Lord say, "France on fire." Within weeks, Notre Dame burned in front of the eyes of the entire world. The devastating fire in France's capital made headlines in Christian and secular media alike. As I reported on this drama for *Awakening* magazine, I was not convinced in my spirit that it was the last strike against France. And so we kept watching and praying.

JUDGE THE WARNING

How do you handle warnings that seem too hot to handle? With the wisdom of God and a good dose of common sense. The first thing I do when I hear a warning of destruction is to judge the warning. There's a disturbing trend in the Body of Christ with new prophetics rising up without much training or understanding of the ways of God or how to judge a prophetic encounter.

What we've seen in recent years is Christians releasing second heaven revelation that is breeding fear in the Body of Christ. A second heaven revelation is something the enemy shows you. It's usually scary and has no hope or redemption in it. Remember, the principalities are raging in the second heaven, whereas God reigns in the third heaven. Revelation from God originates in the third heaven. Revelation from the enemy comes from the second heaven.

Again, second heaven dreams, visions, or voices will offer dire representations of what "God is going to do" or the destruction that is to come without any hope. Second heaven revelation is laced with fear, offers no strategy or way of escape, and knocks the wind out of people. The vain imagination that hits the minds of less-experienced watchmen is, "What's the use of praying?"

Make no mistake, second heaven revelation is not revealing the will of the Lord but the plans of the enemy. Remember, when the Lord gives a warning of destruction His intention is for intercessors to rise up and push it back. God always provides a way of escape (see 1 Cor. 10:13).

LOOK FOR THE REDEMPTION

Next, look—or listen—for the redemption of God. Yes, ultimately there are times when God's judgment will fall. There comes a day when enough is enough and there's no averting God's decision. We see this with Nineveh. God sent Jonah the prophet to release a warning to the ancient city, knowing the king and his people would repent. God was right.

> *Jonah began to enter the city on the first day's walk. Then he cried out and said, "Yet forty days, and Nineveh shall be overthrown!" So the people of Nineveh believed God, proclaimed a fast, and put on sackcloth, from the greatest to the least of them. Then word came to the king of Nineveh; and he arose from his throne and laid aside his robe, covered himself with sackcloth and sat in ashes (Jonah 3:4-6).*

The king took the alarm seriously and issued a proclamation that every person and every animal would enter a time of fasting in hopes of turning away the Lord's fierce anger. As a result, the Lord spared Nineveh—for a season. But Nineveh, like Israel, turned back to its wicked ways and was ultimately destroyed in 612 BC by a Babylonian-led coalition.

While the "France on fire" word was not a warning of judgment, it was a warning of destruction. So my first course in handling a word that's too hot to handle is to find God's underlying plan. In the first France warning, years earlier, God said, "The enemy has marked France for destruction because of its spiritual heritage." But He also gave hope of averting the enemy's plan through intercession and promised to involve Himself in the battle and fight for France.

In my book *Prophetic Protocols & Ethics*, I offer a protocol I titled, "Do Seek God for Redemption Amid Hard Words." I'll share that protocol with you here:

God is a God of redemption. After all, in Christ we have redemption through His blood, and forgiveness of our sins according to His riches in grace (see Eph. 5:7). Over and over in the Bible, we see Scriptures pointing to the redemptive nature of God. Here are just a few to drive the truth home.

Colossians 1:14, "In whom we have redemption through His blood, the forgiveness of sins." And Titus 2:14, "Who gave Himself for us, that He might redeem us from every lawless deed and purify for Himself His own special people, zealous for good works." And "But of Him you are in Christ Jesus, who became for us wisdom from God—and righteousness and sanctification and redemption" (1 Corinthians 1:30).

God is not just a God of redemption under the New Covenant. He has always been a God of redemption. The Old Testament Scriptures prove it. Psalm 111:9 tells us: "He has sent redemption to His people; He has commanded His covenant forever: Holy and awesome *is* His name." And Psalm 107:2 says, "Let the redeemed of the Lord say *so,* Whom He has redeemed from the hand of the enemy."

What does it mean to redeem? The Greek word for *redeem* is *lutroo*. According to *The KJV New Testament Greek Lexicon*, it means "to release on receipt of ransom, to redeem, liberate by payment of ransom, to liberate, to cause to be released to one's self by payment of a ransom, to redeem, and to deliver from evils of every kind, internal and external. God is good. He is a redemptive God."

PRAY BEFORE RELEASING A WARNING

Next, pray into the warning. By that I mean pray and ask the Lord to share more. He may or may not, but sometimes you have not because you ask not. Be spiritually curious and ask the Lord for additional prophetic intelligence that can help you pray more effectively.

With the "France on fire" word, for example, I had very little to go on. How can I take action on a word that I don't know how to apply? So I prayed.

Many times, God shows watchmen information and waits to see if they will ask for more information. Spiritual curiosity is a prerequisite of a successful spiritual watchman. God deems the ones who dig deeper into the prophetic warnings from the Holy Spirit trustworthy to pray and take Spirit-inspired actions on the revelation.

The ones who ask, seek, and knock on the Holy Spirit's door of revelation will get more—if not all—of the prophetic insight they need to see

God's Kingdom come and His will done on earth as it is in heaven. Sometimes, we are on a need-to-know basis with God. He only tells us what we need to know so we don't get presumptuous, overwhelmed, or afraid.

SEARCH AND KEEP ON SEARCHING

Sometimes, our prayer journey will lead us on an investigative journey into the news or world history. When I heard "France on fire," I had no frame of reference for what that could mean. Initially, I pondered the positive side of this expression—being on fire for God. We were in talks to launch an Awakening House of Prayer in France and I hoped this was what God meant, but I knew there was more to it.

I discovered revival wind hit France around 1100 AD through the Albigenses, known as "reformers before the reform." Another group called the Waldenses were evangelistic reformers who took the gospel into Spain, Germany, Poland, and Bohemia.

Of course, we must remember the Huguenots, French Protestants whose numbers rose to about 2 million by 1562 and openly displayed their faith despite persecution. France also saw an awakening in the late 19th century and Pentecostalism spread there in the early 20th century.

France's Christian heritage is indeed rich—and France has seen more than its fair share of terror attacks dating all the way back to Christmas Eve 1800 when a bombing left 22 dead and over 50 injured. All told, there were seven deadly terror attacks in France in the 1800s.

I knew in my spirit, though, this wasn't about revival. As I walked the streets of Paris, round about the area where the Eifel Tower stands in all its majesty, I just could not shake the words "France on fire." As is my custom, when the Lord stops speaking I start seeking. I started research-ing historical fires in France and came up empty. Most of the fires in France are in the last 20 years and two of them were Channel Tunnel fires. What was God saying?

As I walked the streets of Paris, I kept seeing signs protesting President Emmanuel Macron. I saw an economic justice movement and discovered its participants are called Yellow Vest Protestors because they wear yellow vests. I stumbled on news reports of protestors setting fires in France. Just days prior, I discovered Yellow Vest protestors were continuing to set shop fires in what marked the 18th week of unrest in the European nation. News reports indicated France was unprepared for the riots that had ensued. The Associated Press reported:

> French yellow vest protesters set life-threatening fires, smashed up luxury stores and clashed with police Saturday in the 18th straight weekend of demonstrations against President Emmanuel Macron. Large plumes of smoke rose above the rioting on Paris' landmark Champs-Elysees Avenue, and a mother and her child were just barely saved from a building blaze.[1]

I still did not know Notre Dame would burn. But at least I got inter-cessors praying. Notre Dame could have burned to the ground. It didn't. I believe intercession helped save the iconic figure.

WHAT'S THE TIME FRAME?

After all that prayer, I had no time frame on this warning about "France on fire." Was it imminent? Within 30 days from now? Next year? How long did we have to pray against this fire? Sometimes you just don't know. Other times you do. Let me give you an example.

When the Lord started speaking to me at 6:30 in the morning just two weeks before the 2016 Summer Olympics, I wasn't even aware the Olympics were coming down the pike. I was knee deep in my role at *Charisma* magazine. I heard the Lord say:

> ISIS and other dark forces have formed a confederacy that will orchestrate a coordinated attack at the Olympics. The plan calls for attacks on every side and in diverse manners. Suicide bombers are being trained to infiltrate the perimeter with new tools and tactics and with mass carnage in mind.
>
> Even areas in the outskirts of the city will be targeted to bring mass chaos and spread thin responding forces. Demonic alliances are being forged even now because the attacks in the minds of these terrorists surpass the resources any one group has collected on its own.
>
> Underground networks are being formed even now to strike several cities on the same day, even though the Olympics are the primary targets of terror.

I saw fire, lots of fire, and people being trampled as they tried to race away from the sites. I saw chemical weapons being deployed that suffocate victims. Other chemical weapons were deployed that led to a slower, more painful death. It was clear to me that this coordinated attack was not depending or relying on any one method or strategy or group. This was a cadre of groups unified for one evil purpose.

When I researched this out, I discovered the Games in Rio were to run from August 5 to August 21. I also read news reports indicating Brazil had beefed up Olympic security after the Nice terror attack and how security services foiled a French delegation at the Rio 2016 Olympics. In other news, a Brazilian extremist group used the *Telegram* to pledge allegiance to ISIS.

While I understood some of the news may be just chatter, I felt in my spirit some of it was likely real and I was convinced there was much more going on behind the scenes. I still remembered watching in horror the aftermath of the terrorist bomb attack on Centennial Olympic Park in Atlanta during the 1996 Summer Olympics. The attack ultimately killed two people—one immediately and a second had a heart attack while running to the scene—and injured 110 others. In other words, we've seen terror attacks on the Olympics before. Now, in an age of terror when we see violence every week, we need to take this warning seriously.

The timeline on this was two weeks. Two weeks didn't leave us much time to thwart this terror attack. God would not have warned if He did not want to intervene. I chose to believe we could take authority over these demons before the manifest in the midst of a global scene. We rallied intercessors. Within two days, fervent intercession had led to the arrest of 10 people plotting terror on the Rio games. Meanwhile, Brazil police smashed an ISIS plan for attacks on the games. But keep praying. Al-Qaeda is calling for lone wolf terrorists to rise up.

WHEN TO RELEASE THE WARNING

We live in an internet era, a new media age. For all the dangers of social media among emerging prophetic voices who carry great zeal but may lack wisdom in what to share or when to share it, it's critical we do discern when to share and use various forms of media as a vehicle to get a prophetic word, dream, or vision to the masses.

This is especially true when a prophetic revelation carries a warning or a call to prayer. When a prophetic message is urgent, it's vital for as many people as possible to hear the prophet's cry. In the Old Testament, they blew trumpets and sounded alarms at critical junctures. Consider *The Message* translation of Jeremiah 4:5-7:

> *Sound the alarm in Judah, broadcast the news in Jerusalem. Say, "Blow the ram's horn trumpet through the land!" Shout out—a bullhorn bellow!—"Close ranks! Run for your lives to the shelters!" Send up a flare warning Zion: "Not a minute to lose! Don't sit on your hands!" Disaster's descending from the north. I set it off! When it lands, it will shake the foundations. Invaders have pounced like a lion from its cover, ready to rip nations to shreds, leaving your land in wrack and ruin, your cities in rubble, abandoned.*

Not every warning needs to be blazed abroad with urgency, but we must use media to our advantage, including blogs, email lists, social media, radio, mobile apps, group messaging, and so on. I believe if Jesus walked the earth today, He would use media. In fact, God used a form of media—a book—to record His will for the ages. It's called the Bible.

So when do you release the warning? When God tells you to. There are some warnings God may have you release to just a few intercessors who can pray with fervency and confidentiality. This is especially true when the warnings are about individuals in private matters. When the prophet Nathan approached David about his sin with Bathsheba, he did so privately (see 2 Sam. 12:1-14). Other times, the warning needs to be judged by other watchmen and prophets in the Body of Christ. Still other times it needs to be released loudly and as far and wide as possible as quickly as possible.

That was the case in 2016 when I was on my way to the inauguration of President Donald J. Trump. When I flew into D.C., there were so many secret servicemen on the plane I wondered what was going on! I was texting with some colleagues about it when suddenly I looked up, and President Jimmy Carter was standing in front of me, extending his hand so I could shake it. It was an interesting encounter that had me pondering many things.

When I landed in D.C., I got caught up in the Carter entourage but finally made it to my cab. That's when I heard an urgent warning in my spirit over D.C. I heard: "Danger, danger, stranger danger. It's not coming from where you think." I could not shake it. I actually stayed behind in my hotel room, skipping the evening festivities to pray. I discerned it had something to do with an attack on the president's son and sounded the alarm, not with fear but with a sober mind and encouragement that we could push back the darkness. And we did.

Even if you don't have a timeline from the Lord, He can tell you when to release it. You may also feel an urgency in your spirit—like what Jeremiah called fire in his bones (see Jer. 20:9). Past experience working with the Lord helps you discern between fervor in your soul and fire in your bones. It's not always black and white, which is why we can rely on the counsel of elders when we do not know if or when to warn. If it's urgent—if it's about a terror attack or some tragedy—I'd rather release it even if I am wrong than to find out later I was right and did not release it. I do not want the blood on my hands. That said, when we're wrong we have to take responsibility or we'll lose credibility.

DON'T SPREAD FEAR

I can't stress this point enough. If you look for the redemption in the warning, the strategy, or the way of escape, you are less likely to spread fear. Novice watchmen hear the word of the Lord or see what the enemy is doing in the spirit and the spirit of fear comes on them. Then, when they release their warning it is cloaked in a spirit of fear that hits the hearts of the listeners. That does not foster prayer.

If the warning scares you, press into God to get the mind of Christ. God did not give us a spirit of fear but of power, love, and a sound mind (see 2 Tim. 1:7). God gives us warnings because He loves the human race and He wants us to avoid the snare of the enemy. When He warns, He does not do it to spur fear in our hearts. There is no fear in love, and God is love. When He warns, He is motivated by love.

DEVELOP PRAYER POINTS

Once you discern the Lord's direction, it's time to develop prayer points. How can you rally intercessors if you don't give them a clear assignment? You develop prayer points by seeking the Lord's will and His strategy. When possible, use Scripture. Here are the prayer points I developed for the threats of terror on France.

Pray for the hedge of protection to rise up around France. Pray for an end to terror in France. Pray against this constant attack on France's spiritual inheritance; bind the hand of the thief that is working to dampen fervor for another awakening. Pray that intercessors on the land will repent for the sins of the land and work as agents of healing. Pray that the Lord would empower politicians and police with strategies to eradicate terrorists and thwart future attacks. Pray that intercessors in France will not grow weary.

When I was in London shortly after Notre Dame burned, I met a lead intercessor from a prayer network in France who thanked me for sounding the alarm. She had hundreds of intercessors praying. You never know who is going to hear your warning. That's why I release the warning with a solution—specific prayer points that inspire hope and faith that the enemy's plans can be thwarted. If you're always warning but never offering a prophetic solution, you can steal the hope and faith of people.

RELEASE THE WARNING CONFIDENTLY AND WITH DIPLOMACY

Remember, God is looking for people to stand in the gap and make up the hedge to avert destruction. But how can they pray if the watchman doesn't issue the warning? Paul said, "For if the trumpet makes an uncertain sound, who will prepare for battle?" (1 Cor. 14:8). The watchman needs to release the warning with certainty and boldness if he wants anyone to believe him.

The flip side of boldness is diplomacy. What is diplomacy, you ask? *Merriam-Webster's* dictionary defines it as skill in handling affairs without arousing hostility.

As I write in my book *Prophetic Protocols*, being a diplomatic prophet means you are "exactly reproducing the original" and "employing tact and conciliation especially in situations of stress." *Tact* is "a keen sense of what to do or say in order to maintain good relations with others or avoid offense." Delivering words of warning must be done with diplomacy to avoid perceptions of judgment on a person, as if they are in some way to blame, etc.

FORTHTELL OLD WARNINGS

We've spent a lot of time in prophetic ministry foretelling, but forth-telling is also part of prophetic ministry. *Forthtell* means "to make public" or to "publish abroad," according to *Merriam-Webster*'s dictionary. You could also say to "tell forth." One aspect of forthtelling is to say what God has already said. I call it re-prophesying the warning.

There is so much emphasis on predicting in the prophetic realm, and that's valid, but what about prophesying the warning God already gave until people actually hear it? At times, the Lord will have a watchman release a warning from another watchman that was issued a decade ago. John Paul Jackson's Perfect Storm message is a great example. People are re-issuing his warnings, as well as David Wilkerson's. You can re-prophesy the warning. You can keep decreeing it until it lands on ears that hear.

NOTE

1. The Associated Press, "Yellow vest protesters set life-threatening fires and clash with police in Paris," CBSnews.com, March 16, 2019, https://www.cbsnews.com/news/paris-riots-mother-child-saved-from-bank -fire-champs-elysees-avenue-today-2019-03-16.

Chapter 10

WATCH AND PRAY

WHILE the watchman is called to watch—hence the name *watchman*—he is also called to pray. Some say the watchman's job is complete after he releases what he sees. Nothing could be further from the truth. The watchman is called to be part of the solution, to be part of the prayer meeting. And at times, the watchman is the only one praying.

Yes, the watchman's life can be a lonely one at times. The watchman often watches alone and often prays alone. (Though he's not really alone, because the Holy Spirit is with him all the while.) The watchman often eats the scroll alone and then releases a warning that lands on deaf ears. The watchman often sounds the alarm to a sleeping church and makes intercession while the saints are snug in their beds without a care in the world. The watchman's burden in prayer is often severe.

Keep in mind that Ezekiel 22:30 was spoken to the prototype watchman. Consider Ezekiel 22:30 in its context and notice how Ezekiel is not only called to watch but also to pray in the midst of a land ripe for God's judgment. Let's start in verse 23 and go on to verse 31:

> *And the word of the Lord came to me, saying, "Son of man, say to her: 'You are a land that is not cleansed or rained on*

in the day of indignation.' The conspiracy of her prophets in her midst is like a roaring lion tearing the prey; they have devoured people; they have taken treasure and precious things; they have made many widows in her midst. Her priests have violated My law and profaned My holy things; they have not distinguished between the holy and unholy, nor have they made known the difference between the unclean and the clean; and they have hidden their eyes from My Sabbaths, so that I am profaned among them. Her princes in her midst are like wolves tearing the prey, to shed blood, to destroy people, and to get dishonest gain. Her prophets plastered them with untempered mortar, seeing false visions, and divining lies for them, saying, 'Thus says the Lord God,' when the Lord had not spoken. The people of the land have used oppressions, committed robbery, and mistreated the poor and needy; and they wrongfully oppress the stranger. So I sought for a man among them who would make a wall, and stand in the gap before Me on behalf of the land, that I should not destroy it; but I found no one. Therefore I have poured out My indignation on them; I have consumed them with the fire of My wrath; and I have recompensed their deeds on their own heads," says the Lord God.*

You are probably the most familiar with those last two lines—"I sought for a man among them who would make a wall, and stand in the gap before Me on behalf of the land, that I should not destroy it; but I found no one." But understanding the context here helps you understand the connection between watching and praying, even when things seem helpless and hopeless. God is always looking for a man (or woman) to stand in the gap to avert disaster. God doesn't send warnings so we merely brace ourselves for what's coming. He sends us warnings so we can shut the enemy out. Even in the midst of Israel's sin, God was looking for a praying watchman.

ISAIAH: THE TIRELESS WATCHMAN

We can learn plenty about the intercessory prayer function of watchmen by taking a glimpse into the lives of the watchmen in the Bible. The reality is, beyond the prophets who served as watchmen, most of the watchmen in the Bible are not named. We hear of the "young man who was keeping watch" (2 Sam. 13:34) and "the watchman [who] went up to the roof over the gate" (2 Sam. 18:24). We see watchmen reporting (see 2 Kings 9:20). But we can learn some key aspects of praying watchmen in Isaiah, Habakkuk, and Anna.

When you think of a watchman, your mind probably immediately runs to Ezekiel, who is perhaps the most striking example of a watchman due to the Lord's strong words during his calling. We'll be exploring Ezekiel plenty in the pages of this book as he is a prototype. But maybe you don't relate to Ezekiel. Maybe his testimony is a bit too bloody. Or maybe God is calling you to a different expression of the watchman.

While Ezekiel was known for prophesying and attention-getting prophetic acts, Isaiah is perhaps better known for prayer. We gain insight into Isaiah's watchman ministry in Isaiah 62:6-7:

> *I have set watchmen on your walls, O Jerusalem; they shall never hold their peace day or night. You who make mention of the Lord, do not keep silent, and give Him no rest*

till He establishes and till He makes Jerusalem a praise in the earth.

In prayer, the watchman will remind God of His eternal purpose. Beyond Isaiah 62:6-7, we read another passage that seconds the motion in Isaiah 43:25-27:

> *I, even I, am He who blots out your transgressions for My own sake; and I will not remember your sins. Put Me in remembrance; let us contend together; state your case, that you may be acquitted. Your first father sinned, and your mediators have transgressed against Me.*

The watchman as intercessor has compassion and will plead with God for mercy. If this aspect is missing, the watchman is wayward, which means he's following his own inclinations and working against what God expects him to do. The job of the watchman to continue to ask God for His will—and for mercy in the face of judgment—is paramount.

Remember the cry of Habakkuk, another watchman, who wrote, "O Lord, I have heard Your speech and was afraid; O Lord, revive Your work in the midst of the years! In the midst of the years make it known; in wrath remember mercy" (Hab. 3:2). A watchman who doesn't remember mercy is not serving the Lord's purposes. God wants to show mercy, but often we need someone to stand in the gap to request it.

In his role as a watchman, the prophet Isaiah prayed tirelessly. *The Passion Translation* of Isaiah 62:6-7 uses that very word:

> *Jerusalem, I have stationed intercessors on your walls who will never be silent, day or night. You "reminders" of Yahweh, take no rest, and tirelessly give God no rest, until he*

*firmly establishes Jerusalem and makes her the praise of all
the earth!*

Isaiah wasn't just prophesying to the intercessors. Isaiah was one of those intercessors. As the one who receives the prophetic revelation, the watchman should be the first to open up in prayer and the last to utter "amen."

The praying watchman is so sold out to the purposes of God that he will give up life's fleeting comforts to make intercession.

HABAKKUK: A WATCHMAN TO THE NATIONS

Habakkuk was a high-level watchman. You've heard the phrase, "prophet to the nations." Well, Habakkuk was a watchman to the nations. Habakkuk 1:1 starts out talking about the burden the prophet Habakkuk saw. Listen to his conversation with the Lord:

> *O Lord, how long shall I cry, and You will not hear? Even cry out to You, "Violence!" and You will not save. Why do You show me iniquity, and cause me to see trouble? For plundering and violence are before me; there is strife, and contention arises. Therefore the law is powerless, and justice never goes forth. For the wicked surround the righteous; therefore perverse judgment proceeds* (Habakkuk 1:2-4).

The Lord replied, "Look among the nations and watch—be utterly astounded! For I will work a work in your days which you would not believe, though it were told you" (Hab. 1:5). The conversation continues from there, but I wanted to emphasize how Habakkuk was a watchman to the nations. After continuing the conversation with the Lord through the first chapter of his self-named book, Habakkuk was determined to step into the fullness of his calling.

Habakkuk's words, "I will stand my watch and set myself on the rampart, and watch to see what He will say to me, and what I will answer when I am corrected" (Hab. 2:1). In response to this commitment, the Lord answered him and said:

> *Write the vision and make it plain on tablets, that he may run who reads it. For the vision is yet for an appointed time; but at the end it will speak, and it will not lie. Though it tarries, wait for it; because it will surely come, it will not tarry* (Habakkuk 2:2-3).

As a watchman to the nations, Habakkuk was given instructions to write down and publish what he saw. But that wasn't where his responsibility ended. After the Lord continued to share His displeasure with Israel in Habakkuk 2:5-20—citing woes against those who covet evil gain for their house, woe to those who build a town with bloodshed, woe to those who give a drink to his neighbor, and other woes—the watchman went into immediate intercessory prayer action in Habakkuk 3.

The entire chapter is essentially a prayer response and is too long to reprint here, but I encourage you to go read it for yourself. I'll give you what I feel is one of the most important parts: "O Lord, I have heard Your speech and was afraid; O Lord, revive Your work in the midst of the years! In the midst of the years make it known; in wrath remember mercy" (Hab. 3:2). Through the pages of Habakkuk, we see the watchman prophet make calls for repentance, proclaim judgment on nations, and prophesy against the treachery of Jerusalem. But we cling to his watchman prayer: "In the midst of the years make it known; in wrath remember mercy."

ANNA: THE PROPHETIC INTERCESSOR

In the pages of the New Testament, we find Anna. Anna is an expression of Isaiah's prophecy is Isaiah 62:6-7:

> *I have set watchmen on your walls, O Jerusalem; they shall never hold their peace day or night. You who make mention of the Lord, do not keep silent, a give Him no rest till He establishes and till He makes Jerusalem a praise in the earth.*

This was the lifestyle of Anna. We read about her in Luke 2:36-38:

> *Now there was one, Anna, a prophetess, the daughter of Phanuel, of the tribe of Asher. She was of a great age, and had lived with a husband seven years from her virginity; and this woman was a widow of about eighty-four years, who did not depart from the temple, but served God with fastings and prayers night and day. And coming in that instant she gave thanks to the Lord, and spoke of Him to all those who looked for redemption in Jerusalem.*

Anna wasn't looking for demons. Anna was looking for the glory personified. Anna was looking for the Christ. The Anna anointing is an anointing for prophetic intercession. In her book *The Voice of God: How*

God Speaks Personally and Corporately to His Children, Cindy Jacobs writes:

> Prophetic intercession is the ability to receive an immediate prayer request from God and pray about it in a divinely anointed utterance. ...Many times, such prayer requests come in the form of prophetic words. The people praying may not realize this at the time and only later find out it was God speaking to them to pray prophetically. At times when I pray like this, it is not so much that God gives me a lengthy prophecy, but a name will come to me while I am praying. I then open my mouth to pray and trust God to fill it with the word of intercession He wants. Yet on other occasions, I will ask the Lord, "How do you want me to pray for this matter?" and He will give me the next instruction.[1]

OIL THE SHIELDS

"Arise, you princes, and oil the shields." These words from Isaiah 21:5 (MEV) struck my heart in a strong way one morning. "Arise, you princes, and oil the shields." Isaiah uttered these words in response to a "grievous vision" that sent him into travail, perplexed and dismayed him, and caused his heart to beat fast in overwhelming fear. The Bible says he trembled all night long (see Isa. 21:1-5). Imagine receiving such a prophetic vision from the Lord!

"Arise, you princes, and oil the shields." When Scripture leaps off the page, we need to pay attention to what the Lord is trying to show us. In this encounter with the written Word of God, verse 6 also spoke to my heart. It reads: "Go, station a watchman; let him declare what he sees" (MEV).

As watchmen, it's not enough to make petitions. We must also prepare for the spiritual battle in this season. We must step into the watchman's ministry in this hour so we can warn the Body of Christ of impending attacks that will surely come. We must oil the shields or, as another translation puts it, "anoint our shields."

Oil is a symbol of the Holy Spirit. The praying watchman needs fresh oil with which to oil our shields so we don't grow weary. Speaking prophetically, some watchmen have run out of oil in their lamps much like the five virgins in Matthew 25. The Bible calls these virgins "foolish" because they carried their lamps but didn't take oil with them. When the Bridegroom let out a cry at midnight, the foolish virgins awoke and sought to borrow oil from the wise virgins. The wise virgins refused and the Bridegroom ultimately rejected the foolish virgins.

In this parable, Jesus concluded, "Watch therefore, for you know neither the day nor the hour in which the Son of Man is coming" (Matt. 25:13). I don't know when Christ is returning, but I do discern the signs of the times, and He is coming as a "thief in the night" (1 Thess. 5:2).

Beloved watchman, now is not the time to run out of fresh oil. Now is not the time to depend on someone else's relationship with Jesus or someone else's anointing to carry you through the battles that will emerge in the days ahead as you walk in your calling. Now is the time to cultivate the oil of intimacy in your life—to invest in a deeper relationship with the Holy Spirit—so that you can stand and withstand in the evil day. Just as Moses used oil to anoint the priests and consecrate them for service, we need to set ourselves apart to receive His anointing so we can faithfully execute His call on our lives.

In Ephesians 6, Paul lists the whole armor of God but concludes by writing, "And above all, taking the shield of faith, with which you will be able to extinguish all the fiery arrows of the evil one" (Eph. 6:16 MEV). The warfare will grow more intense in this next season. The Holy Spirit is calling us to "oil the shields." The strategy here is not only to meditate on the Word of God to build our faith but also to pray in tongues to oil our shield. Jude 20 tells us, "But you, beloved, build yourselves up in your most holy faith. Pray in the Holy Spirit" (MEV).

The benefits of praying in the Spirit are too vast to list here. However, let me give you a few and encourage you to study this out yourself and discover the benefits through practical experience. Praying in tongues is direct communication to God that the devil cannot comprehend (see 1 Cor. 14:2); activates the fruit of the Spirit (see 2 Cor. 3:18); releases a prayer perfectly in line with God's will; releases understanding into the mysteries of God (see 1 Cor. 14:2); opens up realms of revelation (see 1 Cor. 12:8); and positions you to engage in spiritual warfare from a position of victory (see Eph. 6:18). (You can take "Transform: A 90-Day Spirit Prayer Challenge" for ninety days of lessons on praying in the spirit and what it does for you at schoolofthespirit.tv.)

THE COMING PROPHETIC SEASON

Watchmen, we are coming into a season where we will see "people fainting from fear and expectation of the [dreadful] things coming on the world" (Luke 21:26 AMP). We're seeing a foretaste of this even now. We must invest time to cultivate the oil of intimacy so we can oil our shields as we enter escalating end-times warfare amid a Great Falling Away that will see many deceived.

Yesterday's manna is not going to cut it. We must live by every word that proceeds out of the mouth of God (see Matt. 4:4). We must determine to press into fresh revelation, fresh understanding, fresh anointing—fresh manna. The key word is *fresh*. Stale manna is not going to sustain your faith in the coming season. Some in the body have been taught wrong doctrines and others are believing heresies. We must guard our hearts from these deceptions. Watchman ministry will receive new-found respect in the coming hour as Christians find themselves blind-sided by world events. Watchmen and spiritual warriors will connect in new ways, working together in unity to push back the darkness trying to stop the manifestation of the glorious church. Prophets who have been hidden in the wilderness will emerge with fresh oil on their shields and fresh revelation in their hearts to declare the uncompromising word of the Lord by faith.

A final word for the praying watchman. Remember, as you do the praying God gets the glory. Psalm 127:1 tells us, "Unless the Lord builds the house, they labor in vain who build it; unless the Lord guards the city, the watchman stays awake in vain." This is a sobering Scripture. The Lord is not just a Warrior, He's a Watchman. He watches everything. He has the power to guard the city. So as watchmen we want to cooperate with the grace of God.

NOTE

1. Cindy Jacobs, *The Voice of God: How God Speaks Personally and Corporately to His Children* (Ventura, CA: Regal Books, 1982), 39.

Chapter 11

THE WATCHES OF
THE WATCHMAN

A watchman is always a watchman and can spring into action at any time. But God knows you can't watch and pray twenty-four hours a day, three hundred and sixty-five days of the year. You have to go to work, play with the kids, make dinner, and take care of innumerable responsibilities in the natural realm every week. That's why God assigns watchmen to specific watches.

A watch is a period of time in which God has appointed you to watch and pray. It is one of eight three-hour periods—four in the night and four in the day—where God sets sentinels in the watchtowers to stand guard. Watchmen are assigned to various watches for various reasons.

Though some focus largely on the four that start from 6 p.m. to 6 a.m., there are eight prayer watches. Understanding the time frames of these watches, their significance, and how to operate in those dimensions is part of your making process. Armed with this information, you'll better understand the purpose for your watching.

Your watch can change based on God's need of your eyes to see, ears to hear, voice to pray, and cry to warn. You could be on the first watch one week and the fourth watch the next. Your watch time may also change according to other shifts God is making in your life. Being flexible with God will lead you to revelation you wouldn't otherwise experience and rewards you wouldn't ultimately heap in eternity for faithful service. That said, God will often establish you in one watch for a significant period before moving you to new watches.

THE FIRST WATCH

The first watch runs from 6 p.m. to 9 p.m. This is the first of four night watches and serves as the foundation of the night. The first watch is a time to be still and know that He is God (see Ps. 46:10). In Scripture, we see Isaac meditated on God in the first watch. Genesis 24:63 reads, "And Isaac went out to meditate in the field in the evening; and he lifted his eyes and looked, and there, the camels were coming."

Meditating on God's Word is essential for the watchman. It helps remind us of our covenant with God, prepares us for revelation through dreams and night visions, and prepares us for success in our watchman ministry because we become more sensitive to the presence of God. Jehovah told Joshua:

> *This Book of the Law shall not depart from your mouth, but you shall meditate in it day and night, that you may observe to do according to all that is written in it. For then you will make your way prosperous, and then you will have good success* (Joshua 1:8).

The psalmist wrote, "I will meditate on Your precepts, and contemplate Your ways" (Ps. 119:15). And David said, "When I remember You on my bed, I meditate on You in the night watches" (Ps. 63:6). And again Psalm 119:148 says, "My eyes are awake through the night watches, that I may meditate on Your word." When we meditate in this way, we are more familiar with how God moves in the spirit and are also more likely to discern disturbances in the spirit.

The first watch, then, is as much about preparing the watchman for future watches as it is about watching for danger. The first watch, you could say, is about watching for the Lord, listening for His instructions, renewing your mind to His awesome power and love, remembering your covenant, and readying yourself for what lies ahead.

THE SECOND WATCH

The second watch runs from 9 p.m. to 12 a.m. This watch starts with thanksgiving to the Lord as Protector and petitions for divine intervention in the battle for the coming day. Spiritual warfare marks this watch. The enemy wants to stand against the revelation God is trying to show you about the attack.

This is a time for the watchman to discern and stand against the enemy's onslaught before he even has time to enter formation. The enemy readies to launch his attacks during this watch, so it's vital that the watchmen are stationed on the wall with eyes wide open. The second watch is a time to cry out to God to break in with light to illuminate the enemy's plans.

The watchman's heart's cry in the second watch sounds like this: "Let God arise, let His enemies be scattered; let those also who hate Him flee before Him" (Ps. 68:1). The enemy will try to scatter our attention. Distractions will come to cause you to lose focus on the mission. Your eyes may grow weary as you approach the latter half of the watch.

Remember, Exodus 12:29-31 describes how God passed over the Israelites and struck the firstborn son of every Egyptian family, setting up the ultimate deliverance for Israel. The second watch is a time of miraculous intervention, deliverance, and the overthrow of dark structures in society that keep people captive. At the conclusion of this watch, the watchman's cry sounds something like this, "At midnight I will rise to give thanks to You, because of Your righteous judgments" (Ps. 119:62).

THE THIRD WATCH

Also called "the witching hour," the third watch is from 12 a.m. to 3 a.m. Principalities, powers, rulers of the darkness and spiritual wickedness in high places are overactive during this watch. Therefore, this watch is usually reserved for more seasoned watchmen who are experts in spiritual warfare and understand their authority. Some also call this the cockcrowing watch. During this watch is when Peter denied Christ three times (see John 13:38).

The third watch is marked by witches, warlocks, and satanists who are releasing witchcraft, curses, incantations, potions and spells, and evil decrees over people, governments, cities, and nations. This is a strategic time for dark forces because most of the victims are sound asleep and unaware of the operations, defenseless to fight back. There are fewer intercessors pushing back darkness during this watch. That's why the watchman is posted as a guard to keep the city safe through intercession.

During this time, God may lead you to engage in battle against enemies attacking families, businesses, and churches in your community—or even your own life. Before you set out to pray, plead the blood of Jesus over yourself and claim Psalm 91. If this is not your assigned watch but you sleep during this watch, you may face nocturnal warfare or the enemy may deliver second heaven dreams—that is, dreams showing his plans and purposes with despair and hopelessness following.

The third watch is also the time to command your morning. Consider Job 38:12-15:

> *Have you commanded the morning since your days began, and caused the dawn to know its place, that it might take hold of the ends of the earth, and the wicked be shaken out of it? It takes on form like clay under a seal, and stands out like a garment. From the wicked their light is withheld, and the upraised arm is broken.*

Take authority over your day and command its way.

THE FOURTH WATCH

Also called the morning watch, the fourth watch is from 3 a.m. to 6 a.m. The morning watch is the last watch of the night. Exodus 14:24 speaks of the morning watch:

> *Now it came to pass, in the morning watch, that the Lord looked down upon the army of the Egyptians through the pillar of fire and cloud, and He troubled the army of the Egyptians.*

This is the breaking of the day watch. Some call it the glory watch because it's when the glory of God begins to cover you from enemy sight. Look again at Exodus 14:24, quoted above. During this time, the Lord will trouble the enemy through your prayers in the glory.

> *I wait for the Lord, my soul waits, and in His word I do hope. My soul waits for the Lord more than those who watch for the morning—yes, more than those who watch for the morning* (Psalm 130:5-6).

The fourth watch is where we awaken the dawn. This is where we experience resurrection power over our enemies as they return to hiding before the rising of the sun. It is during the fourth watch that we find deliverance. Jesus walked on the water in the fourth watch and God delivered the Israelites from Egypt in the fourth watch.

Angelic activity marks the fourth watch. Consider Job 22:27-28: "You will make your prayer to Him, He will hear you, and you will pay your vows. You will also declare a thing, and it will be established for you; so light will shine on your ways." As you decree God's will, you establish your day in His presence and angels hearken to the voice of His Word in your mouth to execute His will in your life and the lives of those for whom you are praying (see Ps. 103:20).

THE FIFTH WATCH

The fifth watch is a watch of Holy Spirit preparation that runs from 6 a.m. to 9 a.m. Technically, it's the first watch of the day. When the disciples were filled with the Holy Spirit on the Day of Pentecost, it was during the fifth watch. In Acts 2:14-16, Peter said:

> *Men of Judea and all who dwell in Jerusalem, let this be known to you, and heed my words. For these are not drunk, as you suppose, since it is only the third hour of the day. But this is what was spoken by the prophet Joel.*

The fifth watch, then, is a time to watch for the leading of the Holy Spirit for the day—and to pray for an outpouring of His Spirit in your life, city, and nation. Just as the Holy Spirit poured Himself out on the 120 disciples in the Upper Room, He will do it again. Declare Isaiah 44:3: "For I will pour water on him who is thirsty, and floods on the dry ground; I will pour My Spirit on your descendants, and My blessing on your offspring." Pray for evangelists to be emboldened by the Spirit to be witnesses that Jesus is alive (see Acts 1:8).

In the fifth watch, step into the prophetic spirit and prophesy over your life, prophesy over your family, prophesy over the economy, prophesy over the seven mountains of society, prophesy over businesses, prophesy over cities and nations. The Holy Spirit is pouring Himself out and your response is to pray and prophesy. Write down what He says and use those prophecies to engage in intercession.

Wage war with the prophetic word according to First Timothy 1:18: "This charge I commit to you, son Timothy, according to the prophecies previously made concerning you, that by them you may wage the good warfare." Pray for the Body of Christ to receive a fresh infilling of His Spirit to equip and empower them to do the will of God and resist the attacks of the enemy.

THE SIXTH WATCH

The sixth watch, from 9 a.m. to noon, is a watch when promises are fulfilled. This was the watch during which Jesus was crucified. Jesus hung on a cross at 9 a.m. (see Mark 15:25). This is the watch when God delivers people out of darkness and into His light (see Col. 1:3). It's a time to meditate on the power of the cross, who we are in Christ, and the yes-and-amen promises of God in Christ.

The sixth watch is a time of intercession for lost souls to come out of satan's grip and into the hands of the loving Father through faith in Christ. It's a time to pray for the benefits of our salvation found in Psalm 103:1-5:

> *Bless the Lord, O my soul; and all that is within me, bless His holy name! Bless the Lord, O my soul, and forget not all His benefits: who forgives all your iniquities, who heals all your diseases, who redeems your life from destruction, who crowns you with lovingkindness and tender mercies, who satisfies your mouth with good things, so that your youth is renewed like the eagle's.*

This is a time to pray for the Bride of Christ to willfully crucify her flesh; live, move, and have her being in Him; and be willing to lay aside all self-will for His will as Jesus did in the Garden of Gethsemane when He prayed three times to the Father, "Not My will, but Yours, be done" (Luke 22:42). Like Paul said:

> *I have been crucified with Christ; it is no longer I who live, but Christ lives in me; and the life which I now live in the*

flesh I live by faith in the Son of God, who loved me and gave Himself for me (Galatians 2:20).

THE SEVENTH WATCH

The seventh watch is from noon to 3 p.m. After Jesus gave up His spirit at noon, darkness covered the earth until 3 p.m. This is when Peter and John went up to the temple for the hour of prayer, the ninth hour (see Acts 3:1). This is a time to take authority over the powers of darkness in prayer. Watch for enemy activity in this day division from the secret place.

While darkness is working to overshadow the earth, dwell in the secret place of God and He will hide you under His shadow (see Ps. 91:1). From that place of refuge, you can trust God to give you a vantage point to see the fowler's snare and the deadly pestilence the enemy is planning to release in your midst. His faithfulness will be your shield and buckler as you make intercession against the work of the enemy.

This is a time to get ahead of the enemy's plans to release satanic arrows and disaster in the day and night terrors and pestilence that stalks in darkness. The trouble will not come near you as you dwell in the secret place of the Most High. This is a time when you will gain confidence in your authority as you watch with your eyes the punishment of the wicked.

This is also a time of angelic activity, as angels are dispatched to guard you and those for whom you are making intercession in the secret place. This is the time to boldly tread on demon powers that are treading in your city, understanding Jesus gave you the authority to tread (see Luke 10:19). This is a time God will deliver those for whom you are praying and deliver prayer answers that have lingered.

THE EIGHTH WATCH

The eight watch, which is the last day watch, is from 3 p.m. to 6 p.m. It's sometimes called the history-making watch because Jesus died on the cross at 3 p.m., forever changing history. This is a time to meditate on the blood of Jesus. This is a time to come boldly before the throne of grace to find grace and obtain mercy (see Heb. 4:16). This is the time to make intercession for healing and deliverance made possible by the shed blood of Jesus.

This is a time of repentance, even identificational repentance for cities and nations. Cry out to God for the sins of the land according to Second Chronicles 7:13-14:

> *When I shut up heaven and there is no rain, or command the locusts to devour the land, or send pestilence among My people, if My people who are called by My name will humble themselves, and pray and seek My face, and turn from their wicked ways, then I will hear from heaven, and will forgive their sin and heal their land.*

In this way, your prayers can change the course of a nation's history.

Break curses that have been spoken over you, your family, your cities, the economy, and your nation. Understand Galatians 3:13-14:

> *Christ has redeemed us from the curse of the law, having become a curse for us (for it is written, "Cursed is everyone who hangs on a tree"), that the blessing of Abraham might come upon the Gentiles in Christ Jesus, that we might receive the promise of the Spirit through faith.*

Chapter 12

PITFALLS
FOR WATCHMEN

B EYOND demons and glory, the modern-day watchman has to keep his spiritual eyes open for something else—personal pitfalls. The enemy hates the watchman because, many times, the watchman is the only one to see him coming in to steal, kill, and destroy (see John 10:10). And if the watchman is not the only one who sees the works of darkness approaching, the watchman is often the first to see it and the first to sound the alarm, blow the trumpet, and otherwise blow the devil's cover.

Put another way, the watchman is one of the greatest threats to the kingdom of darkness because of his mantle to watch and pray, his passion for prayer, and his keen discernment. The enemy digs pitfalls in the watchman's path, hoping he will stumble and fall into miry clay. Therefore, the watchman must not only watch in the spirit but must also watch his path, watch his motives, watch his mind, and watch his mouth.

As a prophetic prayer ministry, the watchman's journey is rife with prophetic pitfalls and abuses. The enemy wants to pervert your voice of warning one way or another, and he sets you up for a fall at strategic points on your pathway to maturity. The good news is if you understand the most common pitfalls, stumbling blocks, and deceptions, you are more likely to avoid the enemy's snare.

As I write in my book *Prophetic Protocols & Ethics*, developing strong character will help you avoid the pitfalls, abuses, and even potholes, which are less damaging but can hinder your progress on your watchman's journey. In my experience, I've witnessed many people fall and some get back up again. If we can remove our foot from evil as fast as we recognize the temptation to step into it, we escape the polluting powers of the enemy in our prophetic ministry.

PUSHING PAST MINISTRY PITFALLS

Merriam Webster defines *pitfall* as a "trap, snare, a pit flimsily covered or camouflaged and used to capture and hold animals or men" and "a hidden or not easily recognized danger or difficulty." An *abuse* is a "corrupt practice or custom; improper or excessive use or treatment, misuse; language that condemns or vilifies usually unjustly, intemperately, and angrily; physical maltreatment, or; a deceitful act."

A pitfall in any ministry, but particularly for the watchman, is finding identity in the gift instead of the gift Giver. Our identity should be rooted and grounded in Christ, not in a gift. In your making process, if God sees you are too wrapped up in what you do for Him instead of who you are in Him, He may put you on a shelf for a season to work on identity issues. Remember, when Jesus was in the wilderness satan attacked His identity saying, "If You are the Son of God" (Matt. 4:6). Jesus didn't fall for the temptation because He was secure in His identity as a Son.

When it comes to warnings, being too confident in your gift to let others judge serious warnings before releasing them is a pitfall that can damage your credibility. You don't want to be known in the Body of Christ as the boy who cried wolf, releasing warnings prematurely, incompletely, or from the second heaven and frightening people for no reason. Yes, everybody can miss it, but if you are too proud to submit your warnings to others to judge, then you are setting yourself up for a fall before you even start walking. Pride comes before destruction and a haughty spirit before a fall (see Prov. 16:18).

Positioning yourself as a watchdog instead of a watchman can be tempting if you don't know how to deal with righteous indignation over errors (or what you perceive as errors) you see in the Body of Christ. Watchdogs behave more like dogs that guard a property. They bark at everyone who approaches whether good or bad. A watchdog is typically self-appointed. There are secular watchdogs and spiritual watchdogs. But most watchdogs are not tamed and they can easily slide over into the realm of heresy hunter. Watchdogs may carry a spirit of control or a spirit of criticism or even a spirit of suspicion rather than discernment.

Looking for a devil behind every doorknob at the expense of looking to see what the Lord is doing is a pitfall that can mark you as a dark watchman. Yes, there's a lot of demonic activity. And sometimes there are three devils behind the doorknob, but if you never have anything good to say or if you never see anything good to say, there's something wrong. You may have a bent toward seeing demonic activity, but press in to see the Lord's plan and glory and you will be a balanced watchman.

Going beyond the bounds of your authority is a pitfall that can bring tremendous warfare on your life. Paul wrote, "We, however, will not boast beyond measure, but within the limits of the sphere which God appointed us—a sphere which especially includes you" (2 Cor. 10:13). The Greek word for *measure* in that verse is *metron*, which means a sphere of influence. If you try to take on the entertainment mountain of society but God has not called you there, for example, you may not know how to battle the principalities and powers in that realm and end up with massive backlash for which you are not prepared.

Mistaking the enemy for the Lord or the Lord for the enemy is a mistake young watchman can make. That can be because they aren't seeing clearly in the spirit. It can also be because they don't know how the Lord moves or the ways of His Spirit—or they don't know how the enemy slithers or his sinister devices. Safeguard yourself against this pitfall by being a student of God and His emotions, His ways, His character, His attributes, and comparing that to the ways of the enemy.

Warning presumptuously can bring damage to an individual, the local church, or the larger Body of Christ. Presumptuous means to overstep bounds. Presumption is sort of like assumption in that you see evidence that something is probably true but you don't know that is definitely true. When the Spirit of God shows or tells you something, you won't have to wonder if it's true. Beyond bias, watchmen fall into presumption by putting too much emphasis on natural perceptions, like prophesying blowing wind in the natural correlates to spiritual circumstances (it can, but doesn't always) or they may erroneously apply a dream God intended just for them to the whole church.

The Bible speaks over and again about presumptuous prophets, but you could apply those same verses to presumptuous watchmen:

> *"But the prophet who presumes to speak a word in My name, which I have not commanded him to speak, or who speaks in the name of other gods, that prophet shall die." And if you say in your heart, "How shall we know the word which the Lord has not spoken?"* (Deuteronomy 18:20)

God is not going to strike the watchman dead, but presumption will hinder your eyes, ears, and voice.

Getting the timetables wrong is an issue with watchmen who are hasty in spirit to release a word or feel pressure to put a date on a warning. The Holy Spirit who gave you the warning will give you the timetable. If you don't have a timetable, then don't try to stretch into one. Just wait on the Lord. You can discern a sense of urgency in your spirit when the time is short. Don't be hasty in announcing timelines. Proverbs 29:20 warns, "Do you see a man hasty in his words? There is more hope for a fool than for him."

OVERCOMING PERSONAL PITFALLS

Beyond ministry pitfalls that can stem from immaturity or issues of the soul, there are deep heart issues that can lead you into dangerous territory as a watchman. Sometimes these are unresolved hurts and wounds and inner healing is mandated. Other times, it's wrong teaching and the mind needs to be renewed. Still other times it's demonic oppression and deliverance is required. Still other times it's the flesh and it has to be crucified.

One personal pitfall is the temptation for worldly fame. Remember, the devil led Jesus up to a high place and showed Him all the kingdoms of the world. Jesus wanted us to have a heads-up about one of the devil's most successful tricks—seducing offers of worldly fame, glamour, and riches in exchange for our worship. When watchmen fall, it's often because they got ahead of God's timing in the face of opportunity for fame, glamour, or riches and chose to compromise to get now what God would have given them in the future.

Bitterness in the heart can lead the watchman into witchcraft. Simon the Sorcerer wasn't a watchman, but the gall of bitterness led him into witchcraft practices and his experience serves as a model. Simon was well known for his sorcery, but after he got saved he didn't get healed from the bitterness, and when his magic powers were gone he tried to buy the Holy Ghost. Peter said to Simon, "Repent therefore of this your wickedness, and pray God if perhaps the thought of your heart may be forgiven you. For I see that you are poisoned by bitterness and bound by iniquity" (Acts 8:22-23). Bitterness will defile your warning ministry (see Heb. 12:15). Bitterness is often behind the gloom-and-doom watchmen and prophets and their mouths are full of curses and bitterness (see Rom. 3:14).

Fear of man will bring a snare into the watchman's ministry (see Prov. 29:25). Jesus told His disciples, "And do not fear those who kill the body but cannot kill the soul. But rather fear Him who is able to destroy both soul and body in hell" (Matt. 10:28). When God told Ezekiel the blood would be on his hands if he did not share God's warning with the people, I am sure it put the fear of the Lord in him. I am sure he didn't necessarily enjoy being the warning guy, and he may even have battled fear to speak those words. But the watchman's fear of the Lord must be greater than the fear of man.

Poor relationship skills are a pitfall to the watchman because God did not design the watchman to walk solo. The watchman may watch alone, but to fulfill his assignment he needs to build relationships with other watchmen who can judge a revelation and with intercessors willing to pray something through in private. The watchman must also build credibility with the larger Body of Christ so his voice is heeded. Ecclesiastes 4:9 says two are better than one. Jesus sent the disciples out two by two (see Luke 10:1). One can put a thousand to flight, but two can put ten thousand to flight (see Josh. 23:10).

Being unprepared for the persecution can cause the watchman to abandon his post. Persecution will come. Many people, even Christians, do not like to hear warnings. In Luke 6:22-23, Jesus said:

Blessed are you when men hate you, and when they exclude you, and revile you, and cast out your name as evil, for the Son of Man's sake. Rejoice in that day and leap for joy! For indeed your reward is great in heaven, for in like manner their fathers did to the prophets.

The same truth applies to watchmen who are standing in a prophetic function.

Rejection and pride can go hand in hand and can derail a watchman's ministry as quickly as anything. Paul said knowledge puffs up (see 1 Cor. 8:1). That means knowledge can give you a tendency to get prideful. On the other hand, rejection tears down. These are often two sides of the same coin as people who have rejection can compensate by operating in a pride or a false humility. Remember Solomon's wise words, "When pride comes, then comes shame; but with the humble is wisdom" (Prov. 11:2). You'll have to keep a watch over your soul for pride, because it creeps in as you grow in your anointing and in prominence. If you have rejection issues, you need to study your identity in Christ. You are accepted in the beloved, not because of your role but because He loves your soul (see Eph. 1:6).

STEERING CLEAR OF STUMBLING BLOCKS

Beyond pitfalls, the enemy puts stumbling blocks in the path of the watchman. In order to avoid stumbling blocks, we need to recognize them when they arise along the narrow path. At the most basic level, a stumbling block is an obstacle to our progress in the Lord; it's something that gets in between us and God's perfect plan for our lives; it is anything that leads us into temptation. It's a snare. *Strong's Concordance* defines a stumbling block as "any person or thing by which one is (entrapped) drawn into error or sin."

One of the key stumbling blocks for watchmen (and prophets alike) is having one's own opinion rather than submitting to the Lord's heart. Watchmen should not take on any opinion except God's opinion. Proverbs 18:2 puts it bluntly: "A [self-confident] fool has no delight in understanding but only in revealing his personal opinions and himself" (AMPC). Watchmen need God-confidence and to express God's warning and God's strategy for escaping danger or otherwise seeing His will come to pass in the life of a person, city, region, or nation.

The watchman can become a stumbling block for other people by making an unrighteous judgment. When you watch, you may see things about people that are ungodly. For example, you may see that someone in the church has a Jezebel spirit and is targeting the worship leader. As a watchman, you have to separate the personality from the principality. In other words, you have to learn not to pass judgment on the person but to judge a righteous judgment in the spirit (see John 7:4). Sharing with others what you see about someone in the spirit the wrong way can create a stumbling block to their freedom. Jesus wants to see people set free. If you paint them as the devil, who will want to help them? They will walk out of the church more hurt than when they came in. Wisdom is to warn and proceed with discernment while walking in love. Remember Paul's words in Romans 14:10-13:

> *Why do you criticize and pass judgment on your brother? Or you, why do you look down upon or despise your brother? For we shall all stand before the judgment seat of God. For it is written, As I live, says the Lord, every knee shall bow to Me, and every tongue shall confess to God [acknowledge Him to His honor and to His praise]. And so each of us shall give an account of himself [give an answer in reference to*

judgment] to God. Then let us no more criticize and blame and pass judgment on one another, but rather decide and endeavor never to put a stumbling block or an obstacle or a hindrance in the way of a brother (AMPC).

A righteous judgment is a judgment based on the Word and the Spirit—a judgment that does not condemn a struggling heart. If God gives you a warning about a person, ask Him what to do next. Is this person just an assignment against the church? Is it a witch or some other type of person who has an agenda to cause harm and, therefore, needs to be expelled? Or is this person on whom you see an evil spirit merely seeking deliverance and help and came to your church to get it? Ask God to show you the motive of the heart before you make an unrighteous judgment against the person. Only God sees the motive of the heart.

If someone's steps were ordered by the Lord to your church for help and you sound the alarm in such a way that people withdraw that help, your ministry has become a stumbling block to the Lord. We can warn wrongly based on past experience with a person who looks or talks the same as a troubler in the past. We must go beyond the surface and see the roots before parting our lips.

Many years ago, I served in a ministry that proposed to have great discernment. Some of the prophets and teachers were experts at calling out the demons on people the first time they walked through the church doors. While they may have been right, their lack of love grieved the Holy Spirit. Many people walked in hoping to see transformed lives as promised on the church's website and instead stumbled over the watchman's judgment. The watchman who makes others stumble ultimately stumbles over himself. The watchman's motive must, at all times, be love. First John 2:10 tells us, "He who loves his brother abides in the light, and there is no cause for stumbling in him."

Yes, we can be a stumbling block to the Lord's will. We can be near-sighted in the spirit. Peter was. You may remember the scene, but perhaps you have not considered this in the context of the watchman's ministry. In Matthew 16, we read about Jesus' trip to Caesarea Philippi. He stopped along the way to ask His disciples who people said He was. Only Peter got it right, revealing Jesus as the Christ, the Son of the Living God (see Matt. 16:16). Jesus blessed Him and said he was hearing right from the throne room. But just a few minutes later, Peter became a stumbling block. Let's read Matthew 16:21-23:

> *From that time on Jesus began to explain to his disciples that he must go to Jerusalem and suffer many things at the hands of the elders, the chief priests and the teachers of the law, and that he must be killed and on the third day be raised to life. Peter took him aside and began to rebuke him. "Never, Lord!" he said. "This shall never happen to you!" Jesus turned and said to Peter, "Get behind me, Satan! You are a stumbling block to me; you do not have in mind the concerns of God, but merely human concerns"* (NIV).

Other versions of the Bible translate *stumbling block* as offense, a dangerous trap, a hinderance, in my way, or a scandal unto me. Can you imagine the Lord telling you that you were offensive, a dangerous trap, a hinderance, in His way, and a scandal to His Kingdom? Watchmen will make mistakes. There is a learning curve in any ministry, or you might call it a making process. But we must take care to watch ourselves so we don't stumble and offend the Lord. He is God, and He is the ultimate watchman. When we get rid of our judgment and biases, we can see what He sees and warn with His heart.

Chapter 13

A WORD ABOUT
FALSE WATCHMEN

THERE was once a young shepherd boy who tended his sheep at the foot of a mountain near a dark forest. It was rather lonely for him all day, so he thought upon a plan by which he could get a little company and some excitement. He rushed down toward the village calling out, "Wolf, Wolf!" and the villagers came out to meet him, and some of them stopped with him for a considerable time.

This pleased the boy so much that a few days afterward he tried the same trick, and again the villagers came to his help. But shortly after this a wolf actually did come out from the forest, and began to worry the sheep, and the boy of course cried out, "Wolf, Wolf!" still louder than before. But this time the villagers, who had been fooled twice before, thought the boy was again deceiving them, and nobody stirred to come to his help. So the wolf made a good meal off the boy's flock, and when the boy complained, the wise man of the village said, "A liar will not be believed, even when he speaks the truth."

You probably recognize this story. It's one of Aesop's fables—and it offers plenty of truth. In fact, it serves as a strong illustration for this chapter. With the rapid rise of bona fide watchmen, we have to expect the rise of the immature, presumptuous, and false watchers. I would be doing you a disservice if I didn't warn you about this phenomenon. Not everyone who cries wolf—not everyone who releases a warning—is doing so with accuracy or purity.

Some watchmen are yet immature in the ministry and are premature in their release, bringing fear on the Body of Christ in the process. Others are presumptuous, overstepping their bounds of authority and bringing confusion to many with ill-timed or poorly communicated warnings. Then there are watchmen who are altogether false.

As far back as Isaiah's day, God was warning His people to beware of false watchmen. Isaiah 56:10-11 offers a strong indictment against poser watchmen:

> *His watchmen are blind, they are all ignorant; they are all dumb dogs, they cannot bark; sleeping, lying down, loving to slumber. Yes, they are greedy dogs which never have enough. And they are shepherds who cannot understand; they all look to their own way, every one for his own gain, from his own territory.*

The Bible warns over and again about false spirits and people who operate in them. Jesus said, "Take heed that no one deceives you" (Matt. 24:4) False watchmen have deceived many over the years with date setting and warnings of economic collapse that drove fear in the hearts of mankind. Some best-selling books have been based on bogus warnings that frightened people into purchasing a revelation.

We can learn plenty about false watchmen from the warning in Isaiah. I want to stress there's a difference between a watchman who is learning the ropes or even one who steps into presumption and a false watchman.

That's why books like this are so important. God is raising up a new generation of watchmen, and they need training.

BLIND AS A BAT

False watchmen are blind, figuratively speaking. They can't see what God would show them because they are either not watching or they are puffed up with vain imaginations. That's right, false watchmen often don't watch. They take the title but they don't operate in the function. If they would look, they could be of service to heaven, but they don't watch and pray. Often, false watchmen fabricate visions. Paul warned:

Let no one cheat you of your reward, taking delight in false humility and worship of angels, intruding into those things which he has not seen, vainly puffed up by his fleshly mind, and not holding fast to the Head, from whom all the body, nourished and knit together by joints and ligaments, grows with the increase that is from God (Colossians 2:18-19).

The connotation of blind in this verse also speaks to being unable to discern the signs of the times. Jesus rebuked the Pharisees for not discerning the signs of the times:

When it is evening you say, "It will be fair weather, for the sky is red"; and in the morning, "It will be foul weather today, for the sky is red and threatening." Hypocrites! You know how to discern the face of the sky, but you cannot discern the signs of the times. A wicked and adulterous generation seeks after a sign, and no sign shall be given to it except the sign of the prophet Jonah.' And He left them and departed (Matthew 16:2-4).

If Jesus called the pharisees hypocrites because they didn't discern the signs of the times, how much more so is He grieved with those who presume to be watchmen but are blind to the evil going on around them?

IGNORANCE IS NOT BLISS

You've heard the cliché "ignorance is bliss." Well, that's not at all true in the realm of watching. Watchmen are supposed to see what God is showing them. The Bible calls false watchmen ignorant. Interestingly, the Hebrew word for *ignorant* in this verse is *yada*. According to *The KJV Old Testament Greek Lexicon*, it means "to know, to perceive and see, find out and discern, to discriminate and distinguish."

When I first read that, it startled me. *Merriam-Webster's* dictionary reveals the actual meaning of *ignorant*: "destitute of knowledge or education, lacking knowledge or comprehension of the thing specified, resulting from or showing lack of knowledge or intelligence, unaware, uninformed." In Isaiah 56:10 God is saying the watchman should know, perceive and see, find out and discern, and discriminate and distinguish, but does not.

Ignorance is associated with hardness of heart (see Eph. 4:18). Ignorance is often related to unbelief (see 1 Tim. 1:13). Ignorance leads to sin (see Ezek. 45:20). Ignorance is also connected to foolish people (see 1 Pet. 2:15). God doesn't want us to be without knowledge or comprehension, unaware and uninformed about His Word, His ways, or satan's devices. Hosea 4:6 makes it clear: "My people are destroyed for lack of knowledge." Part of the watchman's responsibility is to release knowledge that helps God's people avert destruction.

DUMB DOGS DON'T BARK

False watchmen are dumb dogs who cannot bark. *Dumb,* in this sense, is not ignorant but the inability to sound the alarm and blow the trumpet. *Dumb* means mute, silent, or unable to speak. False watchmen may issue warnings that come from their presumption, a false spirit, or a wrong motive, but they don't blow the trumpet to signal true warnings from God. *Benson Commentary* reports:

They are also slothful and negligent in instructing the people, and do not faithfully reprove them for their sins, nor warn them of their dangers, nor endeavor to keep them from errors and corruptions in doctrine, worship, and conversation, as they ought to do.

False watchmen don't truly care about the people. They are not serving the people; they are serving themselves—and part of the reason they can't bark is because sleeping dogs don't bark. *Barnes Notes on the Bible* offers this insight:

The idea is that probably of dreaming, or drowsing; a state of indolence and unfaithfulness to their high trust. Perhaps also there is included the idea of their being deluded by vain imaginations, and by false opinions, instead of being under the influence of truth. For it is commonly the case that false and unfaithful teachers of religion are not merely inactive; they act under the influence of deluding and delusive views—like people who are dreaming and who see nothing real.

SLEEPING AND SLUMBERING

False watchmen sleep on the job. While wet-behind-the-ears watchmen may fall asleep through apathy, complacency, witchcraft attacks, or waves of weariness, false watchmen regularly sleep on the job. They may brag about how they are on a third watch, but they are hitting snooze on the spiritual alarms. By compromising with the spirit of the world, these watchmen are more comfortable sleeping through the noise of sin that's erupting all around us.

There are four stages of sleep, and each one is telling when paralleled to the spiritual realm. During stage 1, your eyes are closed and there's a reduction of activity. From a spiritual sense, this activity reduction could be caused by weariness, apathy, compromise, or sin. Our eyes are closed. We don't want to see it—we may even justify it. The good news is it's easy to wake up without much difficulty during stage 1. The bad news is this stage doesn't last long, so the opportunity to shake yourself loose from weariness, apathy, compromise, or sin is short.

Stage 2 is a light sleep. There are peaks and valleys, or positive and negative waves, as the heart rate slows and body temperature decreases. At this point, experts say, the body prepares to enter deep sleep. Catch that! Your heart rate slows and your body temperature decreases. Can you see the spiritual parallel? In stage 2, your heart is not on fire for Jesus as it once was. Your love is growing cold. You are in a dangerous place.

Stages 3 and 4 are called the "deep-sleep stages." This is when you dream; this is when you are disconnected from reality. You don't see things as they really are—or you don't see anything at all. During stage 3 you may sleep-walk. It looks like you're going along with the church crowd, but you are actually sound asleep. In stage 4, voluntary muscles become paralyzed. You may not hear sounds in the waking world or respond to activity in the environment around you. If you are awakened, you may be disoriented.

INSATIABLE GREED

False watchmen have an insatiable greed, as do false prophets. As I wrote in my book *Discerning Prophetic Witchcraft*, the love of money is a root of all evil (see 1 Tim. 6:10). False prophets are usually associated with merchandising the saints—also known as fleecing the sheep, also known as prophetic pickpocketing.

Put another way, false prophets (and watchmen) are all about the money, money, money, money. Yes, it takes money to do ministry, but people who pursue ministry for money are ill-motivated and open themselves up to the temptation to bow to the so-called "almighty dollar" instead of the Almighty God.

False prophets aggressively market false miracles, offer manipulative prophetic words, and fabricate testimonies to steal your hard-earned money out of your pocket. These wily workmen operate in hype rather than anointing. We see false prophets merchandising people in the Old and New Testaments:

> *Her leaders judge for a bribe, her priests teach for a price, and her prophets practice divination for money* (Micah 3:11 MEV).

> *But there were also false prophets among the people, just as there will be false teachers among you, who will secretly bring in destructive heresies, even denying the Lord who bought them, bringing swift destruction upon themselves. And many will follow their destructive ways, because of whom the way of truth will be blasphemed. And in their greed they will exploit you with deceptive words* (2 Peter 2:1-3 MEV).

When anyone is focused more on money than on Jesus, it should be a red flag to you. Yes, ministries have to take up offerings. But when people start calling out specific amounts in exchange for specific breakthroughs and blessings, know that something is wrong. You can sow a faith seed, but you can't buy a blessing. Jesus paid the price so you don't have to.

SELFISH AND SELF-CENTERED

False watchmen are selfish and self-centered. Isaiah 56:11 says, "They all look to their own way, every one for his own gain, from his own territory." All believers are supposed to be selfless toward the Lord—and one another. Philippians 2:4 says flat out: "Let each of you look out not only for his own interests, but also for the interests of others." If we're all supposed to watch out for each other, how much more so the watchman who has an anointing to watch and warn?

Selfishness is a sign of the times. Paul wrote in Second Timothy 3:2-5:

> *For men will be lovers of themselves, lovers of money, boasters, proud, blasphemers, disobedient to parents,*

unthankful, unholy, unloving, unforgiving, slanderers, without self-control, brutal, despisers of good, traitors, headstrong, haughty, lovers of pleasure rather than lovers of God, having a form of godliness but denying its power. And from such people turn away!

WRONG MOTIVES

Beyond greed, false watchmen have wrong motives ranging from control to platform to preeminence and the like. The watchman's motive should be love for God and His people. Any other motive is dangerous. Remember the boy who cried wolf? His motive was to get attention.

Philippians 2:3 warns us, "Let nothing be done through selfish ambition or conceit, but in lowliness of mind let each esteem others better than himself." Our watchman ministry should please God even if it doesn't please man (see 1 Thess. 2:4). Service to the King and His Kingdom should motivate our watching and praying.

FULL OF PRIDE

False watchmen, like anyone else, can get puffed up in pride because knowledge puffs up (see 1 Cor. 8:1). Watchmen see things others don't see, and pride can follow. But perhaps the most troubling manifestation of pride in a watchman is a refusal to be reasoned with. The prideful watchman cannot be told he is wrong in what he saw, or how he interpreted it, or his intercession strategy.

VIOLATE SCRIPTURE

A false watchman may report sights that don't line up with Scripture. Of course, everything the watchman sees won't necessarily be found in Scripture. But it should not violate the principles of Scripture. Scripture is a watchman's friend. It helps him find intercessory prayer strategies to stand against the works of darkness.

Chapter 14

WATCHMAN ACTIVATIONS

VERY watchman needs to activate and exercise the gift and learn how to flow in the grace and anointing of God at his station. These watchman activations aim to help you move in different facets of the watchman gift with practical application. With these activations, you can start deploying your watchman anointing now.

First, a word on how to use these activations, which you'll notice are all based on Scripture. Start by setting yourself apart in your prayer room, prayer closet, in your prayer chair, or wherever is your set station to watch and pray. Climb up into your watchtower and be still. By that I mean remove all distractions, calm your mind, and engage in activities like worship or reading of the Word that will bring you into His presence.

You'll notice some of these activations, like the morning watch or night watch, are intended to be done at certain times of the day. Others, such as "Go About the City," are intended to be done in a certain location. In that case, you'll have to leave your prayer chair for an on-location station to complete the activation.

Once you are settled in, read one of the activations appropriate to the time of day, setting, or goal, and ask God to show you what you need to see. Get a journal and write down what you see and hear.

ASK GOD TO HELP YOU BE SERIOUS AND WATCHFUL

In First Peter 4:7 we read, "But the end of all things is at hand; therefore be serious and watchful in your prayers." The watchman can grow weary at times or feel like taking a spiritual vacation, especially after seasons of spiritual warfare. God will give you times of rest, but as a watchman you must always be willing to report for duty whether or not it's convenient. If the Holy Spirit is showing you something, He's showing you so you can take a specific action. This is a sober calling.

Pray this prayer:

> Father, in the name of Jesus, help me to stand serious and watchful. Help me not to grow weary in watching but help me to become more alert and more energized as I stand in Your will at my watchtower. Help me to continue to watch and pray while I am awake and even while I am dreaming.

WATCH AND PRAY FOR ONE HOUR

When Jesus was in the Garden of Gethsemane, He asked His disciples to watch and pray with Him for one hour. In Matthew 26:40 we read, "Then He came to the disciples and found them sleeping, and said to Peter, 'What! Could you not watch with Me one hour?'" Three times, they failed to watch and pray.

Jesus set a standard for watching an hour. Have you ever wondered, "Why one hour?" There are many schools of thought on that. Here's mine: One hour represents a spiritual discipline. As you master the one-hour watch, you are building your strength to watch and pray for extended periods of time. Think about walking on a treadmill. When you are out of shape, you may only be able to walk 15 or 20 minutes. But when you build up your endurance, you can walk an hour or more. Start disciplining yourself to watch one hour.

Pray this prayer:

> Father, in the name of Jesus, help me to watch with the Holy Spirit for one hour. The Holy Spirit is always watching. Teach me to endure in my post long enough to outlast the enemy's attempts to hide from my spiritual eyes. Teach me to endure in my post long enough to see Your glory coming from afar.

ENGAGING IN THE MORNING WATCH

The morning watch is the fourth watch. This is the watch that awaits the dawning of the new day. This watch occurs between 6 a.m. to 9 a.m. Remember, one of the aims of this watch is to discern and hear what the enemy may be doing to spoil the day.

The morning watch is mentioned several times in Scripture, including Exodus 14:24:

Now it came to pass, in the morning watch, that the Lord looked down upon the army of the Egyptians through the pillar of fire and cloud, and He troubled the army of the Egyptians.

You will find interesting spiritual dynamics in the morning watch. During this time frame, the enemy works to sabotage the day before it ever gets started. Remember, Saul sent messengers to David's house to kill him in the morning (see 1 Sam. 19:11). We have to learn to command our morning (see Job 38:12).

Pray this prayer:

> Father, in the name of Jesus, help me station myself at the morning watch as one who is fully awake to what the enemy has planned for the day. Show me the enemies of the cross that are arrayed to steal, kill, and destroy. Position me to stand in the gap to make up hedges the enemy is working to break through so I can thwart the assignment. Help me see what You have planned so I can come into agreement with Your will and Your Kingdom.

If you see the spirit operating, name the spirit and bind it. If not, just push back the darkness that's trying to encroach on the daylight.

NAVIGATING NIGHT WATCHES

The night watches run from 6 p.m. to 6 a.m. These are the first, second, third, and fourth watches you read about in "The Watches of the

Watchman." Psalm 119:148 reads, "My eyes are awake through the night watches, that I may meditate on Your word." And Psalm 63:6 says, "When I remember You on my bed, I meditate on You in the night watches." The night watches have various purposes, from stilling your soul to engaging in warfare against powers of darkness.

Pray this prayer:

> Father, in the name of Jesus, I dedicate myself to You in the night watches. Like David, I will still my soul and meditate on Your Word. Empower me to see through gross darkness into the enemy's plans so I can stand in the gap and make up the hedge to lock him out. Help me not to shrink back from the adversity I find in the night watches but to stay steady until the day breaks.

GO ABOUT THE CITY

The Bible speaks of watchmen who go about the city in Song of Solomon 3:3 and 5:7. You may have heard of prayer walking; well, you can do prayer watching just the same. Drive around your city and begin to watch. You can do this at any time of the day or night. That is, you can combine the morning watch (or any watch) with going about the city.

Pray this prayer:

> Father, in the name of Jesus, as I go about the city alert me to anything that is lurking in the shadows so I can stand against it. Help me see Your plans and purposes for the city, so I can stand in agreement. Give me fresh insight as a watchman into the goings on that most don't see so I can pray without ceasing.

DEVELOP YOUR CRYING OUT SKILLS

Crying out is a skill you need to develop. It goes back to releasing the warning. In Second Samuel 18:25, "Then the watchman cried out and told the king." Before you get to a place where you cry out to the king, cry out to some of your intercessor friends to see how they receive the warning.

Let them judge it and, if necessary, help you shape your language before you report the warning to someone in authority. If you lose credibility with a leader, you could wind up in a situation where people don't believe your warnings and bad things result from ignoring the warning. Crying the right way is a skill. Master the tactics in Chapter Nine.

Pray this prayer:

> Father, in the name of Jesus, help me master the art of crying out. Help me move with a diplomatic spirit when diplomacy is required and with an urgent spirit when urgency is demanded. Teach me how to deliver a warning in the way people will hear it and act upon it.

CALLING TO THE GATEKEEPER

Second Samuel 18:26 reads, "Then the watchman saw another man running, and the watchman called to the gatekeeper and said, 'There is another man, running alone!' And the king said, 'He also brings news.'" Watchmen and gatekeepers need to work symbiotically.

Who is the gatekeeper in your church? The head intercessor, head prophet, or someone who works very closely with the set man or set woman of the church. Until the watchman gains credibility with the leadership of a congregation, you will have to report to the gatekeeper and the gatekeeper will decide if and when the leadership receives the warning.

You can build a good relationship with the gatekeeper by respecting their position. They are guarding the leader from hearing information at the wrong time. Don't try to go around the gatekeeper. Work with them. Earn their trust so they will be more inclined to share your warning.

Pray this prayer:

> Father, please help me adhere to proper protocol in working with the gatekeepers who have the power to share my warnings with leaders who make strategic decisions. Give me wisdom in cooperating with the gatekeeper so that they will hear the words you have put in my mouth and handle them with care.

GROWING IN WATCHING DISCERNMENT

It's important to discern what you see in the spirit. Many Scriptures offer illustrations of watchmen reporting what they saw. It was critical that they report the right information. If they said one man was coming when it was five, the gatekeepers would not be ready. If they saw someone walking when they were running, the gatekeepers might not have the urgency to prepare. Consider these Scriptures:

> *So the watchman said, "I think the running of the first is like the running of Ahimaaz the son of Zadok." And the king said, "He is a good man, and comes with good news"* (2 Samuel 18:27).
>
> *Then Absalom fled. And the young man who was keeping watch lifted his eyes and looked, and there, many people were coming from the road on the hillside behind him* (2 Samuel 13:34).

And the watchman went up to the roof over the gate, to the wall, lifted his eyes and looked, and there was a man, running alone (2 Samuel 18:24).

Now a watchman stood on the tower in Jezreel, and he saw the company of Jehu as he came, and said, "I see a company of men" (2 Kings 9:17).

So the watchman reported, saying, "He went up to them and is not coming back; and the driving is like the driving of Jehu the son of Nimshi, for he drives furiously!" (2 Kings 9:20)

Pray this prayer:

> Father, in the name of Jesus, help me grow in watching discernment. Help me discern clearly whether there's a friend or foe approaching. Give me the clarity of sight to see rightly and report rightly so we can prepare rightly.

WATCH YOUR MOUTH

Beyond watching in the spirit, there's another gate of which you need to be careful—your mouth gate. Psalm 141:3 pleads, "Set a guard, O Lord, over my mouth; keep watch over the door of my lips." As a watchman, you have to know when to cry aloud, know when to report what you see to gatekeepers and kings—and know when to keep your silence.

You don't want your mouth to tip your hand to the enemy. You don't want to share the information you've picked up in the spirit with someone who might mishandle the revelation. It's not always the right time to release what you see. Many of the things you see need to be prayed through before they are spoken out. Learning to hold your peace is a sign of watchman maturity.

Another side of this issue is gossip, slander, idle speech, and corrupt communication coming out of your mouth. If you want to be an effective mouthpiece for the Lord as a watchman, you need to keep your mouth off other people, be careful not to share your opinion in the name of the Lord, or otherwise speak words that grieve the Holy Spirit.

Pray this prayer:

> Father, in the name of Jesus, set a guard over my mouth. Keep watch over the door of my lips. Help me to think before I speak and to speak Spirit-inspired words. Help me not to be rash, judgmental, or critical with the words of my mouth but instead to edify Your people and warn them in a right spirit.

WATCH AT THE GATES OF THE CITY

Proverbs 8:34 says, "Blessed is the man who listens to me, watching daily at my gates, waiting at the posts of my doors." There are gates in any city and some watchmen are assigned to those gates. What are the gates? Think about it practically before you think about it spiritually. A gate is an entrance or a door. Airports and seaports are gates because things come in and out. Courthouses can be gates because legislation is ruled in. Major universities can be gates because ideologies are entering minds.

There are also spiritual gates or portals. Jesus said the gate of hell shall not prevail against the church (see Matt. 16:18). Where are the gates of hell represented physically in your city? In Amsterdam, it would be the red-light district. In Central Florida, it's an old witches' town called Cassadaga. Wherever you see a concentration of evil, the gates of hell are trying to prevail against the church in the city. This is where it's strategic for the watchman to partner with the gatekeepers in prayer at the gates.

There are also godly gates. Psalm 24:7 says, "Lift up your heads, O you gates! And be lifted up, you everlasting doors! And the King of glory shall come in." So we are not just watching for evil at the gates; we are watching for the King of Glory.

Pray this prayer:

> Father, in the name of Jesus, help me discern the spiritual gates of the city. Help me to understand the dynamics and importance of the gates and gatekeepers so we can partner together to shut down the enemy's plans. Help me see the coming of the King into our midst so we can welcome in the King of Glory.

KEEP WATCH ON THE EVIL AND THE GOOD

Proverbs 15:3 tells us, "The eyes of the Lord are in every place, keeping watch on the evil and the good." And Psalm 37:32 says, "The wicked watches the righteous, and seeks to slay him." I want to reemphasize here that watchmen are to watch for evil and good. This has to be reemphasized because the watchman can become demon-focused and miss what God is doing.

As you watch, if you see evil, keep looking until you see good. Read Daniel 7, in which he has a dramatic encounter with evil. He keeps seeing evil, but he keeps on looking until he finally sees the Lord. By contrast, if you are a watchman who only ever sees glory, keep looking until you see the enemies of glory that are seeking to disrupt people's attention or focus on Him. Although we may have a bent one way or another as watchmen, we want to walk in a balanced expression of our ministry and see all the angles so we can pray thoroughly.

Pray this prayer:

> Father, in the name of Jesus, help me see the evil and the good. Help me not to be so mesmerized with evil that I turn away before You show me Your solutions and strategies for the evil that is lurking. Help me not be ignorant to the devil's devices to disrupt Your plans and purposes in the earth by not standing long enough on the watchtower to see the entire landscape.

WATCH OVER YOUR HOUSEHOLD

In your household, you are a gatekeeper. You decide what comes in. The enemy is roaming about like a roaring lion seeking someone to devour (see 1 Pet. 5:8). You must watch over your household and keep the gates locked to approaching enemies. Proverbs 31:27 says, "She watches over the ways of her household, and does not eat the bread of idleness." As watchman, if we can't watch over our household, the Lord cannot trust us to watch over His household.

Pray this prayer:

> Father, in the name of Jesus, help me to watch over the ways of my household. Help me to squash enemy attempts to infiltrate my home with accursed objects, gossip, foul entertainment, or dark powers in the atmosphere. Help me teach others in my household to watch and pray so that our dwelling is secure and filled with Your glory.

SET WATCHMEN IN PLACE

In a corporate setting, you will need to set watchmen in place. This activation may not pertain to you if you are not in a leadership position. But the principle is nevertheless valid and it's vital you understand it.

Nehemiah understood the importance of having watchmen set in place. Nehemiah 4:9 reads, "Nevertheless we made our prayer to our God, and because of them we set a watch against them day and night." In Isaiah 21:5-6 we read:

> *Prepare the table, set a watchman in the tower, eat and drink. Arise, you princes, anoint the shield! For thus has the Lord said to me: "Go, set a watchman, let him declare what he sees."*

In Jeremiah 51:12, we find these instructions:

> *Set up the standard on the walls of Babylon; make the guard strong, set up the watchmen, prepare the ambushes. For the Lord has both devised and done what He spoke against the inhabitants of Babylon.*

Pray this prayer:

> Father, in the name of Jesus, help me to recognize the watchman gift on Your people so I can activate and deploy them to their proper assignments. Help me to choose the right watchmen for the right post. Help me to steward the watchmen you've sent me with wisdom so they can flourish in their role and be an asset to Your Kingdom.

WORK WITH THE WATCHERS

Daniel mentions the watchers three times in Scripture.

> *I saw in the visions of my head while on my bed, and there was a watcher, a holy one, coming down from heaven* (Daniel 4:13).
>
> *This decision is by the decree of the watchers, and the sentence by the word of the holy ones, in order that the living may know that the Most High rules in the kingdom of men,*

gives it to whomever He will, and sets over it the lowest of men (Daniel 4:17).

And inasmuch as the king saw a watcher, a holy one, coming down from heaven and saying, "Chop down the tree and destroy it, but leave its stump and roots in the earth, bound with a band of iron and bronze in the tender grass of the field; let it be wet with the dew of heaven, and let him graze with the beasts of the field, till seven times pass over him" (Daniel 4:23).

The watchers are angels. As watchmen, you need to learn to cooperate with the ministry of angels on assignment. When we speak the Word by inspiration of the Spirit, angels hearken to that Word to execute it in the earth (see Ps. 103:20). You can go deeper into this teaching in my School of Prayer and Intercession at schoolofthespirit.tv.

Pray this prayer:

> Father, in the name of Jesus, give me a sensitivity to the presence of angels so I know when they are in my midst on assignment. Inspire my spirit to release Spirit-inspired words that the angels can pick up and war with. Teach me how to receive and cooperate with the ministry of angels.

BLOW THE TRUMPET

> *But if the watchman sees the sword coming and does not*
> *blow the trumpet, and the people are not warned, and the*
> *sword comes and takes any person from among them, he is*
> *taken away in his iniquity; but his blood I will require at*
> *the watchman's hand* (Ezekiel 33:6).

In the natural, you have to learn to blow a trumpet. Well, technically anybody can blow it, but if you want anyone to be willing to listen to it, you need to learn the dynamics of blowing the trumpet to make a clear sound. Paul wrote these weighty words: "For if the trumpet makes an uncertain sound, who will prepare for battle?" (1 Cor. 14:8).

It takes skill to blow the trumpet with clarity as to inspire a call to action rather than fear. It takes practice to blow the trumpet in such a way that it carries credibility and authority among those whom the sound is intended to inspire. Listen and watch how mature watchmen release warnings.

Pray this prayer:

> Father, in the name of Jesus, give me the courage to blow the trumpet loudly so that the warning reaches all those for whom it's intended. Help me to blow the trumpet with clarity so that people can understand precisely what You are saying. Help me develop my trumpet-blowing skillset by learning from those who went before me.

WATCH OVER THE NATIONS

Habakkuk 1:5 reads, "Look among the nations and watch—be utterly astounded! For I will work a work in your days which you would not believe, though it were told you." Habakkuk was a watchman over the nations. You may not have that same calling, but you may be called upon to watch over nations in specific situations.

Go to Google News and look at the world news. If something strikes your spirit or moves your heart, climb up in your watchtower, be still, and watch. When you're watching, write down what you see about and in nations. That will inform your intercessory prayer going forward. God will be exalted in the nations (see Ps. 46:10). If nothing else, you can pray that Psalm 46:10 prayer as reality over a nation.

Pray this prayer:

> Father, in the name of Jesus, teach me to watch over the nations like Habakkuk did. Stir my heart toward nations that You are assigning me to in any given season. Help me climb to that height in the watchtower that I can see into the nations in the spirit and pray for Your exaltation, Your will, and Your Kingdom to come with confidence and authority.

WATCH TO SEE

> *I will stand my watch and set myself on the rampart, and watch to see what He will say to me, and what I will answer when I am corrected* (Habakkuk 2:1).

Being a watchman doesn't make you a seer, but many watchmen will step into that seer anointing as the Lord wills for His purposes. Remember, every believer has the capacity to see in the spirit. (Check out my book *The Seer Dimensions*.)

As you climb up in your watchtower, ask the Lord to give you a seer's anointing. Be still and intentional about truly looking in the spirit realm. You may have to close your eyes and get in a quiet place with no distractions if you've never done this before. For 101 seer activations, check out my book *Seer Activations*.

Pray this prayer:

> Father, in the name of Jesus, open my seer's eyes so I can see clearly in the spirit what You want to show me. Help me enter into the seer dimensions legally, through Your Spirit, and not be deceived by familiar spirits. Help me learn to navigate the seer dimensions as I stand on my watch.

EYEING THE FOURTH WATCH

The fourth watch is from 3 a.m. to 6 a.m. The fourth watch is where we awaken the dawn. This is where we experience resurrection power over our enemies as they return to hiding before the rising of the sun.

> *Now in the fourth watch of the night Jesus went to them, walking on the sea* (Matthew 14:25).
>
> *I wait for the Lord, my soul waits, and in His word I do hope. My soul waits for the Lord more than those who watch for the morning—yes, more than those who watch for the morning* (Psalm 130:5-6).

Pray this prayer:

Father, in the name of Jesus, help me wait on You in this early watch that ushers in the break of dawn. Help me to tap into the breaker anointing to spoil the plans of the enemy so that the King of Glory can have His way in my day and in my city. Give me a love for the fourth watch.

WATCH FOR WARFARE

Praying always with all prayer and supplication in the Spirit, being watchful to this end with all perseverance and supplication for all the saints (Ephesians 6:18).

And First Peter 5:8 tells us:

Be well balanced (temperate, sober of mind), be vigilant and cautious at all times; for that enemy of yours, the devil, roams around like a lion roaring [in fierce hunger], seeking someone to seize upon and devour (AMPC).

While you are watching, watch for spiritual warfare. Be intentional on seeing into the enemy's plans. Don't walk in paranoia or the "devil behind the doorknob" mentality. This is just an activation exercise. It's especially helpful when you are feeling a stirring in your spirit that the devil is lurking, but any time you watch it's good to watch out for what the enemy has up his sleeve.

Pray this prayer:

> Father, in the name of Jesus, help me watch and see the spiritual warfare brewing in the second heavens so I can sound the alarm. Help me be well-balanced as a watchman, temperate, sober of mind, vigilant, and cautious in the spirit realm. Show me his plans to seize upon and devour so I can blow the trumpet with clarity and urgency.

ALLOW GOD TO WAKE YOU TO WATCH

"Therefore let us not sleep, as others do, but let us watch and be sober" (1 Thess. 5:6). Although Paul was speaking of spiritual slumber, this also translates to natural slumber. At times, God will wake you up to watch and pray. Remember how the disciples Peter, James, and John kept falling asleep in the Garden of Gethsemane even after Jesus asked them to keep watch with Him? We don't want that to be us.

When the Lord gives us a charge to watch, we must be willing to rise up from our slumber—even if we stay in our pajamas—and watch with Him. You can be assured when He wakes you from restful sleep to stand on the night watch that He will show you something significant and He will make up for the sleep you lost supernaturally.

Pray this prayer:

> Father, in the name of Jesus, help me not to roll over and hit the spiritual snooze button when You are calling me to rise up and watch with You. Help me cultivate the discipline and sensitivity to the Spirit to watch with You in the night, even when I am in a dead sleep. My spirit is willing but my flesh is weak.

PRACTICE BEING WATCHFUL IN ALL THINGS

A watchman is a watchman all the time. You don't turn it on or turn it off. It's your vocation. In Ephesians 4:1, Paul the apostle urges us to walk worthy of our calling. That means being watchful in all things at all times. Second Timothy 4:5 admonishes us, "But you be watchful in all things, endure afflictions...fulfill your ministry."

This means to be watchful at work. It means to be watchful driving around. It means being watchful in church. You never stop watching. You never allow your eyes to grow dim. Consider *The Passion Translation* of Ephesians 4:1: "As a prisoner of the Lord, I plead with you to walk holy, in a way that is suitable to your high rank, given to you in your divine calling." As a watchman, you have a high rank and a divine call.

Pray this prayer:

> Father, in the name of Jesus, help me to be watchful in all things. Help me practice the spiritual craft You have entrusted me with perseverance and purity. Help me endure the afflictions of the watchman's vocation.

ABOUT THE AUTHOR

JENNIFER LECLAIRE is the senior leader of Awakening House of Prayer in Fort Lauderdale, Florida, founder of the Ignite Network, and founder of the Awakening Blaze prayer movement. She formerly served as the first female editor of *Charisma* magazine and is a prolific author of more than 25 books.

You can find Jennifer online or send her an email at info@jenniferleclaire.org.

Destiny Image Books by Jennifer LeClaire

Discerning Prophetic Witchcraft

Your End Times Prayer Secret

Victory Decrees

The Seer Dimensions

The Spiritual Warrior's Guide to Defeating Water Spirits

CPSIA information can be obtained
at www.ICGtesting.com
Printed in the USA
BVHW090919211221
624598BV00002B/143